Diving and Snorkeling Guide to

Belize

Includes **Lighthouse Reef, Glover Reef,** *and* **Turneffe Island**

D0390181

Franz O. Meyer

Pisces Books®
A division of Gulf Publishing Company
Houston, Texas

Acknowledgments

Many more individuals than can be listed here contributed during the writing of this guide. All information they shared unselfishly and support or hospitality they offered are gratefully acknowledged, whereas the friendships we developed along the way remain treasured. I am especially pleased to single out and recognize Frank and Joyce Burek, Joan Conklin, John Leek, B. K. and Dale Moore, Earl and Laura Meador, Hugh Parkey, Victoria Showler, and Tatnal Starr III, whose excellent photographs better capture the colorful life of Belize and help bring a wealth of additional information to this guide.

This guide was reviewed by the author
and reprinted September 1995.

 **Pisces Books®**
A division of Gulf Publishing Company
P.O. Box 2608
Houston, Texas 77525-2608

Pisces Books is a registered trademark of Gulf Publishing Company.
Printed in Hong Kong

10   9   8   7   6   5   4   3

Library of Congress Cataloging-in-Publication Data

Meyer, Franz Oswald.
   Diving and Snorkeling Guide to Belize: Lighthouse Reef, Glover Reef, and Turneffe Island/Franz O. Meyer.
      p.   cm.
   ISBN 1-55992-033-5
   1.Skin diving—Belize—Guide-books.   2.Belize—Description and travel—1981- —Guide-books.   I. Title.
GV840.S78M49   1990
797.2′3′097282—dc20   90-32933
                                                                      CIP

Front cover photo courtesy of Burt Jones/Maurine Shimlock of Paradise Expeditions.

Table of Contents

How To Use This Guide

This guide was written to familiarize you with the location and general characteristics of the principal dive sites of Lighthouse Reef, Glover Reef, and Turneffe Island in Belize. Approximate dive site positions are shown on maps. Installation of a mooring system is underway and buoys help you find reefs on your own. However, you will not be required to find reef sites when diving with local boat service. Dive sites are announced on arrival and this guide will give you an idea of what to expect about currents, depth, visibility, bottom topography, and marine life. The information will be a valuable guide in planning both your activity and a no-decompression dive.

I have organized this guide by atoll and reef position relative to prevailing northeasterly winds. Lighthouse Reef dive sites are described first, followed by those on Glover Reef and Turneffe Island. Within each section, I describe dive areas on the protected western reefs before those on the exposed eastern side of each atoll. The east side of each atoll faces directly into prevailing trade winds, so weather determines if you can dive the windward reefs.

The Rating System For Divers And Dives

My suggestion of the minimum level of expertise required for a dive should be taken conservatively, keeping in mind the old adage about there being old divers and bold divers but few bold old divers. In the context of this guide a *novice* is someone in decent physical condition who has recently completed a basic certification diving course, or who has not been diving or has no experience in similar waters. An *intermediate* is a certified diver in excellent physical condition who has been diving actively for at least a year following a basic course and has been diving in similar waters. An *advanced diver* is someone who has completed an advanced certification diving course, has been diving recently in similar waters, and is in excellent physical condition. You will have to decide if you are capable of making any particular dive, depending on your level of training, experience, physical condition, and water conditions at the site. Remember that water conditions can change at any time.

It is vitally important that you honestly assess your diving skills when diving the tremendously steep and deep drop-offs for which the coral atolls of Belize are noted. Although many walls crest between 30–40 feet (10–13 meters), wall diving will increase your average depth greatly. Excellent water clarity and visibility will make deep dives seem much shallower than they really are at many of the sites. So even experienced divers should monitor closely their depth, time, air supply, and decompression throughout every dive.

Most Belize dive destinations have walls that permit divers to experience the thrilling sensation of soaring in space. (Photo: J. Burek.)

1

Overview of Lighthouse, Glover, and Turneffe Atolls

Origin of the Atolls

Lighthouse, Glover, and Turneffe atolls remain somewhat of a geologic frontier in terms of their origin. There are few geologic studies on the vast lagoons, sparkling white cays, and miles of lush reefs that define the atolls, and even less is known about their foundations. What is known suggests these Caribbean atolls did not originate like those found throughout the Pacific.

None of the coral atolls originated by growing around volcanoes. They are flat-topped and there is no geologic evidence for the former existence of volcanoes. Instead, drop-off reefs, a lens-like reef configuration, submarine topographic features, and the rock composition suggest the coral atolls originated on top of giant fault blocks. Faults, which had a combination of up-down and sideways movement on a scale of thousands of feet, bound these features. Although no longer active, earth movement along the faults and reef growth contributed to the development of deep drop-offs all around the atolls. Many drop-offs are deeper than 10,000 feet (3,000 meters).

Rock information from deep boreholes on the atolls offer additional information about how the coral atolls evolved. Several types of rocks not related to volcanic activity make up the foundations of the limestone atolls. Igneous and metamorphic rocks similar to those found in the Maya Mountains form the atoll's core beneath thousands of feet of limestone. They are the deeply buried remnants of a segmented land ridge on which the limestone atolls were built more than 70 million years ago. At that time, the sea began to rise around the uplifted segments. First, there were steep-sided islands and later there were local shoal areas as an ancestral sea advanced across the uneven topography.

Reefs and lagoons did not form until a much later time. Their history dates back 20 million years and is recorded in a limestone graveyard formed by the skeletal remains of ancient coral, algae, and lime-producing organisms. The stack of skeletons is now nearly 6,000 feet (1,800 meters) thick and stands as mute testimony to the longevity and productivity of the coral atolls. Except for being smaller and having somewhat different types of reef-builders, the original atolls differed little from those we see today.

Skeletal remains of red algae, one of many different organisms that contributed to the atoll's growth for the past 60 million years.

Belize forms part of the coast of the Western Caribbean Sea between Mexico and Honduras.

History of the Atolls

Given today's ease of travel, the sense of remoteness that can be experienced is extraordinary when visiting Lighthouse Reef, Glover Reef, or Turneffe Island. Surely the atolls were lost to civilization for a long time. But history shows this is not so.

Maya Indians probably were the first to discover the atolls. If they discovered all of the atolls or what names they may have given them remains a mystery, but archaeologists believe the Maya found out about these offshore reefs while paddling out to sea in search of new trade centers. Today, remnants of ancient Mayan "shell-maidens" (piles of sea shells and rocks) still mark their trade passages through the eastern reefs of Turneffe at Calabash Cay and Northern Bogue area. Evidently, the Maya trade routes extended eastward beyond Turneffe, but Mayan artifacts similar to those found on Turneffe are unknown on Glover and Lighthouse atolls.

The recorded history of the atolls' names begins in the sixteenth century as Spain, England, Portugal, and the Netherlands were eagerly building their empires. From 1528–1532 Spanish explorers searching for riches discovered and charted the coastline and offshore reefs of Belize and Yucatan. In

Looking west across the Mangrove Cays toward the Gulf of Honduras, the Maya Mountains can be seen in the distance about 15 miles (24 km) from the coast. Rocks found there are like those that form the foundations of the three offshore atolls.

Belize is famous for its giant yellow tube sponges. (Photo by J. Burek.)

competition with England for the New World, Spain treated its knowledge of the coast and reefs a military secret. Original names given to the coral atolls are now clouded by confusion and only names published much later remain in use today. Spanish charts released decades after their making show Turneffe used to be called "Terre Nef," Lighthouse reef "Quattro Cayos," (four cays), and Glover Reef "Longorif."

The English, making and publishing their own but poorly detailed maps, named the atolls Glover, Four Cays or Eastern Reef (Lighthouse), and Turneffe in the 1750s. The origin of the name "Glover" is as interesting as it is uncertain. Consensus has it the atoll receives its name from a pirate who claimed the atoll for himself. Considering that pirates were wiped out in the Caribbean before 1750, this fellow may well have been willingly overlooked by England as long as he menaced only Spanish ships. In their struggle with Spain over territorial sovereignty, England would welcome such help.

When England routed a Spanish invasion force off St. George's Cay in 1798, it brought stability and a lasting heritage to the territory. English names given to the atolls and cays in the middle 1700s became permanently established. Only construction of the lighthouse on Half Moon Cay resulted in the Eastern Reefs being renamed "Lighthouse Reef."

The Coral Atolls Today

Much like their names, the coral atolls today have changed little from what they were like when they became a British Colony (British Honduras) in 1862. With little fresh water and limited land areas, they remain sparsely inhabited and wild. There are no major settlements, but scattered cultural features and domestic animals maintain a few permanent and numerous seasonal inhabitants on some cays. For these people, living conditions are simple and private. Pigs and chickens roam freely among stands of coconuts, water is collected in huge vats, because ground water is either of poor quality or limited amounts, and accommodations consist of small homes or one-room huts. Electrical power is generally not available.

As in the past, life on the atolls is intimately tied to the sea. Fishing for conch, lobster, or crab is the main source of income. It is a hard but profitable business for most permanent residents on the atolls.

Natural sponge farming is another venture, but it is not the lucrative business it used to be at the turn of the century. The industry once supported several permanent residents on Turneffe. Now, only one farm remains active on Calabash Cay. Disease and intense competition from cheaply produced synthetic sponges are largely to blame for the demise of extensive sponge plots in Southern Lagoon. Remnants of these can still be found hidden among the line of mangroves surrounding Southern Lagoon.

Coconut farming is another venture from the past that continues these days on the atolls. Plantations, once meticulously maintained by permanent residents, have since succumbed to neglect. Coconut trees today grow wild on many cays and are harvested by seasonal inhabitants of the atolls.

Large heads and platy growths of boulder coral form the main framework of the reefs. ▶
(Photo: F. Burek.)

A large eighteenth-century anchor salvaged from the British wreck Yeldham offers a historic note outside the Fort George Hotel entrance. It reminds us of seafaring men who gave their lives during the development of a nation.

2

Accommodations and Conditions

Although opportunities are limited for staying on the atolls, current interest in diving and water recreation are fueling the development of resorts. Visitors wishing to stay offshore now choose among four different locations. Four resorts became operational in 1990. A long-established resort is located on Turneffe Island's southern end, and another on the eastern reef line of Glover. A third establishment became operational on Glover's Southwest Cays in 1988, and Lighthouse Reef has a new resort on its north end as of late 1989. All are small, personal, and remote, but they offer land-based diving access to the spectacular marine life of the atolls.

Chartered air or boat service is how visitors can reach the resorts from the mainland. Air service currently is available only for the resort on Lighthouse. All other resorts require a 2–6-hour boat transfer.

Atoll Resorts

Turneffe Island Lodge is nestled among the palms of Cay Bokel on Turneffe's southern point. It has a small dive shop and several boats with varying capacities to support your diving needs on and offshore. Although specializing in Turneffe dive sites, those of Lighthouse and Glover Reef are within easy reach.

Two resorts are located on Glover Reef. Glover Reef Atoll Resort resides in a forest of coconut palms and the 20 acres of sparkling white sand on Long Cay. Located on the windward reefs, it offers day boat and unlimited beach diving of shallow walls or patch reefs to no more than 8 divers at a time. Divers wishing a simple experience unencumbered by modern conveniences will enjoy this resort. Meals are often eaten with the Lomont family in a rustic environment. Accommodations are very private in small quaint bungalows that have detached bathrooms.

Manta Reef Resort is a new facility opened late in 1988. It is a full-service dive facility located on South West Cays, which form the southernmost point of the windward reef tract. Like the other two resorts, accommodations are in simple but comfortable bungalows on a private island.

Turneffe Island Lodge gives divers easy access to world class reefs from Cay Bokel. (Photo: H. Parkey.)

Lighthouse Reef Resort is the newest facility to open its doors to divers on the offshore atolls. It is located on Big Northern Cay at the north end of Lighthouse Reef, an area that was rarely available to divers before now. Although still under construction, Lighthouse Resort is operational. It offers exploratory diving and unpretentious accommodations for 4.

An airstrip still under construction will soon make this facility much more accessible than it is now. Once finished, charter flights can trim nearly five hours off the time it takes to reach the resort from the mainland by boat.

People wishing to stay at these resorts must make reservations. Accommodations are limited and visitors require private boat service from Belize City, Dangriga, or Sittee River to the resort. Transfers may take 2–6 hours with favorable sea conditions and may be impossible on some days.

Boat Services

Located 30–60 miles (48–97 kilometers) off the mainland coast, all the coral atolls can be reached only by boat. Several types of boat service are available from the mainland and Cay Caulker located on the barrier reef. Choices range from day boat service from Cay Caulker to dive charters of a week or more on live-aboards out of Belize City and Moho Cay.

Dive boats vary in carrying capacity and schedules. Crewed yachts and some live-aboards will take small groups of 4 or 6, or large groups, to the popular sites. The live-aboards also offer custom cruises to explore new and infrequently visited reefs or focus on seasonal spectacles like whale shark expeditions.

Most dive charters have one or more divemasters to assist you. Divers may be accompanied by divemasters on their first dive or guided on special deep dives such as the Blue Hole, but the rest of the time they may enjoy complete freedom to explore the reefs alone with their dive buddy. Those who wish to be accompanied by a divemaster need only ask.

The Belize Aggressor *is just one way divers can reach and enjoy the distant offshore atoll reefs. (Photo: E. Meador.)*

Weather and Water Conditions

A truly tropical paradise, Belize weather is consistently pleasant throughout the year. Its air temperature is mild, generally hovering between 75–89°F (24–30°C). On the coral atolls trade winds bring almost constantly easterly breezes that keep the days pleasant even during hot summer days.

Significant changes in this kind of tropical weather can occur anytime with the advent of storms. Hurricanes may destroy the tropical bliss during the summer, but in Belize they occur on an average of less than one in every six years. A more frequent weather change that also affects diving adversely develops in the winter. Between November and February arctic cold fronts may push into Belize from North America. These bring "northers," strong north winds and cold temperatures. Passage of the fronts disturbs weather for a day to a week and creates rough seas and generally very difficult or even impossible diving conditions.

Water conditions normally vary only slightly throughout the year. In winter the water temperature may dip to 79°F (26°C) and in summer it reaches 84°F (29°C). Many dive these waters without any form of wet suit, but I find an ⅛-inch shortie in the winter season and a lycra suit (skin) for summer most comfortable for single tank dives. I would even recommend an ⅛-inch farmer-john or full wet suit to those divers planning to make repetitive dives for a full week.

Water visibility varies seasonally and consistently between the windward and leeward side of the atolls. It may be as low as 25–50 feet (8–24 meters) behind the atoll when seas are rough, but most often it is greater than 100 feet (30 meters). Visibility is almost always 100–150 feet (30–45 meters) on reefs along the windward side.

Beneath the afternoon sun, a gentle tropical breeze stirs a cluster of coconut palms on Half Moon Cay to whisper a timeless tale. Little has changed since the lighthouse was built and its keeper enjoys the unhurried and private life established a century ago. (Photo: D. Moore.)

Foreign Exchange

Currency. Much like you find in Caribbean countries, two types of currency are in circulation in Belize—U.S. dollars and the official Belize currency, Belize dollars. U.S. dollars are readily accepted, but change from purchase made in U.S. dollars generally is made in Belize dollars. The official exchange rate varies at banks, but the unofficial exchange everywhere else is 2 Belize dollars for every U.S. dollar. Belize currency is issued in colorful denominations of $1 (green), $5 (red), $10 (black), $20 (brown), and $100 (blue); whereas coin denominations range from 1, 5, 10, 25, and 50 cents.

Shopping. Shopping opportunities are lacking on the coral atolls and limited opportunities are available on the mainland. Belize artisans excel in elegant zericote and cow-horn carvings and in jewelry made from black coral, pearls, conch, and zericote. Straw-hats, woven baskets, and other handicrafts are also available at the Cottage Industries, the National Craft Center, and various workshops. Mayan design dresses and hand-made wall, table, and floor mats made of marking thread are also found in gift shops. You are strongly encouraged to get your souvenir and craft pieces from a store or workshop run by the Belize Tourist Bureau.

Built on the delta of the Belize River, Belize City is a busy port. Almost everyone and everything entering and leaving Belize passes through the city including divers whose destination is the offshore atolls.

Customs and Immigration

A valid passport is required for entry into Belize. Proof of citizenship with other forms of identification such as birth certificate, driver's license or voter's registration, will not be recognized by Belize immigration officials. Also, visitors arriving by air may soon be required to have a return or onward ticket.

Getting through customs can be a crowded and taxing experience now. The customs area is small, crowded, and quite stuffy on hot and humid days. A new airport terminal is under construction and scheduled for completion in 1990. It promises to improve on many of the existing difficulties.

Good divers will always make a three minute safety stop at ten feet on every dive. (Photo by J. Burek.)

3

Diving the Coral Atolls

Miles of unspoiled and varied reefs far removed from population centers make diving the coral atolls a rewarding experience. The three atolls feature a reef system whose length rivals the Belize barrier, the second largest barrier reef system in the world. Almost 140 miles (225 kilometers) of coral reef surround the three atolls and thousands of patch reefs dot the lagoons of Lighthouse and Glover Reef. Together, the atoll barrier and patch reefs offer hundreds of dive sites, but only a small fraction are visited on a regular basis.

Dive operators have selected specific sites because they provide consistently good and varied dives that can be easily accommodated during regularly scheduled charters. Popular dive sites on most itineraries include shallow wall, broken reef, and spur and groove reef diving with optional stops to dive or snorkel lagoon patch reefs or the Blue Hole on Lighthouse Reef. Most are locally well known and are named to reflect a distinguishing feature. However, not all names are firmly established for sites. Different dive operators may call the same reef by dissimilar names because excellent dive locations are kept a guarded secret.

Although specific dive sites are commonly named after local reef variations, most areas are really not different reef types. Rather, they are part of a continuous reef line whose profile varies locally. Significant profile changes typically occur only over distances on a scale of miles and between reefs of the windward and leeward side. Perhaps the most dramatic changes in reef appearance are those seen on Turneffe Island.

A typical dive on the leeward side of Turneffe evokes the following images. The dive boat anchors about a mile (1½ kilometers) seaward from a line of mangrove islands. Nowhere can waves be seen breaking on reefs, but halfway to the mangroves, choppy seas are replaced by flat water. After entering the water, a gradually sloping bottom becomes visible 30–50 feet (10–15 meters) below the surface. Large and small formations of coral are scattered across a white sand bottom. Some coral growths have 10–20 feet (3–6 meters) of relief. A lush garden of soft corals decorates the sand flats and discontinuous coral formations as far as the eye can see. Seaward and beyond the range of visibility, the slope descends more precipitously before assuming a nearly vertical orientation. In some areas the crest of the coral wall occurs above 100 feet (31 meters), elsewhere the coral and sand slope

Belize diving means walls crowded with colorful sponges, decorative soft corals, and fresh growths of stony coral. It also means rich invertebrate and fish life as these organisms enjoy exposure to the open sea and protection provided by the lush reef growth. (Photo: L. Meador.)

extends downward to depths of 180 feet (55 meters) before there is an abrupt transition into very deep water.

On the windward side of Turneffe, dive operators generally anchor their boats near the end of a sloping reef front that extends 300 to 1,500 feet (100 to 458 meters) beyond a distinctive reef crest breaker zone. Looking down from the surface, a well-defined system of living reef ridges separated by sand channels can be seen 30 to 60 feet (9–18 meters) below. An abrupt break in slope terminates the sand channels and living coral formations and marks the position of a vertical wall. In most places the wall extends to depths greater than 1,000 feet (304 meters) with only minor interruptions.

Because Glover, Lighthouse, and Turneffe have only a limited number of small islands that are quite distant from the walls, most dive destinations are almost exclusively made by boat. Beach diving is possible from a few cays, but the entrances and exits are difficult because of an abundance of shallow coral growth and rough seas.

4

Lighthouse Reef

Of the three offshore atolls, Lighthouse Reef is the most popular with dive boats. Half Moon Wall and Blue Hole are perhaps the best known, but a host of other dive sites along the southwestern limb of the atoll offer exceptional diving. Most are located off the western coast of Long Cay. Six sites—Tres Cocos, Long Cay Ridge, Que Brada, Cathedral, Silver Caves and the Aquarium—are regular stops for most of the live aboards.

DIVE SITE RATINGS

Lighthouse Reef

	Novice Diver	Novice Diver and Instructor/Divemaster	Intermediate Diver	Intermediate Diver and Instructor/Divemaster	Advanced Diver	Advanced Diver and Instructor/Divemaster
1. Hat Cay Drop-off	X	X	X	X	X	
2. Tres Cocos	X	X	X	X	X	
3. Long Cay Ridge	X	X	X	X	X	
4. Que Brada	X	X	X	X	X	
5. Cathedral Reef		X	X	X	X	
6. Silver Caves		X	X	X	X	
7. The Aquarium		X	X	X	X	
8. Nurse Shark Lodge		X	X	X	X	
9. Eagle Ray Wall		X	X	X	X	
10. Southwest Cut		X	X	X	X	
11. West Point I & II	X	X	X	X	X	
12. Half Moon Wall		X	X	X	X	
13. Blue Hole					X	

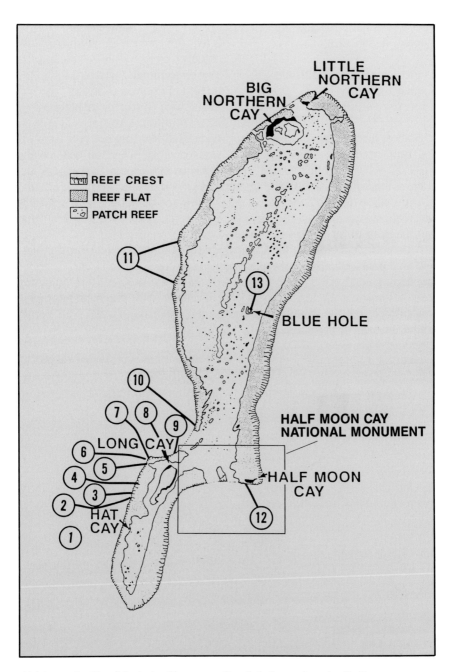

LITTLE NORTHERN CAY

BIG NORTHERN CAY

REEF CREST
REEF FLAT
PATCH REEF

11

13

BLUE HOLE

10

7   8

9

HALF MOON CAY NATIONAL MONUMENT

6   LONG CAY

4   5

2   3

HAT CAY

1

HALF MOON CAY

12

Lighthouse Reef has little dry land but many miles of shallow reefs and walls. Some destinations are within the boundaries of Belize's Half Moon Cay National Monument. (This map is a line trace based on a NASA shuttle photograph.)

Typical depth range:	50 feet (15 meters) to unlimited (wall)
Typical current conditions:	None to minimal
Typical visibility:	50 feet (15 meters) or more
Expertise required:	Novice with instructor or better

A short distance west from a tiny island called Hat Cay is a reef drop-off that bears its name. This drop-off is situated along the main wall on the western limb of Lighthouse Reef. It also has an interesting shallow reef and is the southernmost site dive boats regularly visit on this atoll.

The shallow reef is wide and an extensive patch of sloping sand separates two reefs: a very shallow reef near the island and a narrow line of reefs that hug the drop-off at 50 feet (15 meters).

Although reefs close to the Cay offer excellent snorkeling opportunities, few dive boats actually go there. Instead, dive boats typically anchor above the sloping sand areas close to the wall. Both the drop-off and adjoining reefs offer some exciting diving with dramatic wide-angle photographic possibilities, but the sandy slope behind the reef rimming the wall should not be ignored. It has some unique marine life.

Tattered body of a basket sponge serves as a grim reminder of how much damage a single diver with improper buoyancy can inflict on the reef. (Photo: F. Burek.)

Being almost invisible against the background of a deep-water lace coral helps this clingfish survive being eaten. (Photo: F. Burek.)

Basket Sponges. Along the rim of Hat Cay Drop-off are some huge basket sponges. These must rank as some of the biggest in Belize. The largest of these is quite capable of completely hiding a diver. Whenever divers see such grandeur, most feel the need to climb inside the cavernous sponge opening. However, sponges that have taken a long time to grow invariably get damaged by fins, tanks, or hands during such maneuvers. Damaged sponge tissue is susceptible to diseases that can spread to eventually kill the sponge.

Basket sponges are also home for many other animals and their rough exterior surface should be checked over carefully. Brittle starfish by the hundreds are quite common, but during the day most hide in the deep pits of the sponge. Often, only a few hairy starfish arms can be seen wrapped around the many knobby external sponge growths. Look here for several kinds of gobies or several pairs of white antennae that belong to red and white coral shrimp.

Other Marine Life. The drop-off also has several other major marine life attractions. It has an abundance of deep-water lace coral, giant yellow tube sponges, and there are lots of fish. You may have to do several dives here to appreciate everything this site has to offer.

Typical depth range:	30 feet (9 meters) to unlimited (wall)
Typical current conditions:	Minimal to moderate
Typical visibility:	80 feet (24 meters) or more
Expertise required:	Novice with instructor or better

Named for a cluster of three tall coconut palm trees due east on Long Cay, this reef lies about 1 mile north of Hat Cay Drop-off. It is the second of a series of superb dive sites found on the main western reef line of Lighthouse. Unlike the straight drop-off at Hat Cay, divers can choose from several different attractions. First is a shallow coral reef and wall with some large overhangs. Algae covers much of the shallow reef, but the disappointment of seeing a poorly developed reef is replaced by a satisfying collection of other marine life. Large spotted moray eels, lion's paw sea cucumbers, several kinds of urchins, coral shrimp, arrow crabs, and sea feathers are just some examples of the invertebrates that seek refuge on the reef here. Cowfish scull

Divers taking a close look at the shallow reefs will discover many unusual invertebrates hidden among the coral growth. (Photo: J. Burek.)

Honeycomb cowfish are notoriously poor swimmers and those at Tres Cocos let you get close enough to see their horns. (Photo: F. Burek.)

around patches of coral and juvenile jackknife-fish stay close to the protective holes found everywhere on the reef. A host of damselfish, parrotfish, and blue tang are attracted by the algal lawn to this reef, and schools of jacks share the water above the reef with very large and hungry black groupers.

Divers can spot still more marine life on the wall. Black coral bushes develop on the wall at 30 feet (9 meters). Turtles are common visitors, coming here to graze algae on the sloping sand slopes, and Spanish mackerels and creole wrasses look for food just off the wall.

Following the wall northward, divers will discover large sand flats replace the reef and a wall enhanced with beautiful coral arches 30 to 40 feet (9–12 meters) below the surface. Conch, rays, and peacock flounders are the main attractions on the sand flats. Graceful tube sponges and delicate soft corals hang elegantly from the arches and wall. At 45 to 65 feet (14–19 meters) below the surface, divers can find small schools of black cap basslets close to or under the overhangs. On exceptional days, this part of Tres Cocos offers some of the most dramatic underwater photography possibilities found anywhere in Belize.

Typical depth range:	40 feet (12 meters) to unlimited (wall)
Typical current conditions:	Minimal
Typical visibility:	80 feet (24 meters) or more
Expertise required:	Novice with instructor or better

Long Cay Ridge is the third in a series of excellent walls and shallow reefs off the western side of Long Cay. It receives its name from a protruding ridge of reefs that form a small promontory just a short distance north of Tres Cocos. Spur and groove formation are well defined here on the bottom leading to the wall and a drop-off of major proportions. The grooves run perpendicular to the wall and feed directly into the open sea.

Marine Life. The sponges, coral, and fish seen here are about the same as those on Hat Cay Drop-off. Near the drop-off and all along the wall are many large and colorful sponges and delicate gorgonians. Beneath the canopy

Stony coral growths form overhangs that always have a collection of soft coral and sponges that add interest to wall photographs. (Photo: J. Conklin.)

At a depth of 45 feet (14 meters) on Long Cay Ridge, divers can find arrow blennies such as this one swimming with bent tail among coral recesses on the wall.

of soft coral, tube and vase sponges are fresh growths of boulder, yellow pencil, and finger coral. Deep parts of the wall are shingled with large plates of sheet and sunray coral. Wire coral and small feather black coral trees are other growth on the deep wall. Look among the coral recesses for spotted filefish, arrow blenies, crabs, and lobsters. Threespot and dusky damselfish will charge you if you get too close to their algal gardens along the reef top. This is another place along the Long Cay wall where your searching will reward you with some great photographic subjects.

Typical depth range:	40 feet (12 meters) to unlimited (wall)
Typical current conditions:	Minimal
Typical visibility:	80 feet (24 meters) or more
Expertise required:	Novice with instructor or better

If you move .5 mile (1 km) north of Long Cay Ridge you will come to a small reentrant in the reef known as Que Brada or broken reef. This is another great dive site. Here, a narrow ridge of corals rims a crescent-shaped wall. As elsewhere off the west side of Long Cay, the wall is vertical to slightly overhanging. At about 130 feet (39 meters) a narrow sandy terrace littered with coral provides the only respite on its plunge to unexplored depths. Most dive boats anchor in one of several large sandy areas that interrupt the otherwise continuous coral growth just south of the reentrant. Divers entering the water will see abundant isolated stacks of coral scattered across the sandy bottom, beneath the boat. The coral patches extend right up to the wall which, if followed north just a short distance, turns abruptly to the east.

A deep-water brittle star (Astropopa annulata) *clings tenaciously to a soft coral perch with its bifurcating arms. (Photo: J. Burek.)*

Some live-aboards feed the fish at Que Brada and divers entering or exiting the water may find themselves surrounded by yellowtail snappers eager for a handout.

Fish Feeding Station. Like elsewhere off Long Cay, coral and sponge growth provide plenty of interesting photography and color, but the most exciting photo subjects are friendly and varied fish. Live-aboard dive boats have been feeding fish here for several years now. Schools of yellowtail snappers shadow divers on the reefs. Large black groupers, ocean triggerfish, and a host of others are abundant on the shallow wall and reef crest. Virtually all can be approached, fed, and photographed without much difficulty. Large spotted eagle rays and turtles also frequent the wall of this dive site.

Que Brada also has a collection of unusual invertebrates. These together with friendly fish make this a delightful dive for the photographer who is looking for an unusual picture.

Typical depth range: 30 feet (9 meters) to unlimited (wall)
Typical current conditions: Minimal
Typical visibility: 50 feet (17 meters) or more
Expertise required: Intermediate or better

Cathedral reefs start shallow with the wall cresting at 30 feet (9 meters). Unlike other parts of the Long Cay reef system, those at Cathedral are deeply segmented. Sculptured by and rising above the glistening sand channels are colorful coral spires and formations, with shapes that have inspired the name Cathedral. Divers will find exploring the top of the reef a rewarding experience especially when descending among the coral towers. Here are great narrow passages and short tunnels besides some interesting and different marine life.

Peterson's cleaning shrimp will dance and whip their antennae back and forth as part of a recognition ritual preceding all cleaning activity. (Photo: F. Burek.)

One of the many reef nooks at Cathedral is the lair for a chain eel who makes a living by surprising prey who believed themselves safe inside the system of reef tunnels and holes. (Photo: J. Leek.)

Marine Life. Macrophotographers will love Cathedral. A lush coral garden adorns the reef top and a collection of sponges paint the deep parts of each coral stack red and orange. Healthy growths of boulder, brain, and large plates of cactus coral make excellent photographic subjects. Sea anemones are varied and spread their tentacles out from protective coral nooks. Many act as protective hosts for little spotted brown and Peterson's spotted cleaning shrimps. A varied and friendly fish population adds to the spectacle. Fish watchers will take delight with large French angels, stoplight parrots, trumpets, groupers, and schools of yellowtail snappers. The angels and snappers are particularly easy photographic targets and will readily eat from your hand.

Beyond the shallow reef, large sheet coral up to 6 feet (2 meters) across mantle the wall. Here, huge basket, rope, and long yellow tube sponges add form and grace to the rocky wall. Wire coral, deep-water lace, and other soft coral form elegant growths that extend up to 5 feet (2 meters) from the wall. Look for turtle and lobster among the living cover on the wall. Also keep an eye on the deep parts of the reef below you and on the open sea for large pelagics, such a eagle rays and huge groupers or jewfish.

Typical depth range:	40 feet (12 meters) to unlimited (wall)
Typical current conditions:	None to minimal
Typical visibility:	80 feet (24 meters) or more
Expertise required:	Intermediate or better

Just north of Cathedral, the reef forms a promontory. Unlike other points, the reef here is shallow and deeply segmented, but it is the coral development that sets this site apart from all others. Huge coral formations form a framework riddled with cavities that make excellent hiding places for animals trying to escape their predators. This dive site's name was inspired by the huge schools of silver sides that were found regularly inside the caves. They were a spectacle to behold, but unfortunately, these fish have not been seen in the caves for the past few years.

Cave Dwellers. The absence of silver sides does not totally diminish the attractiveness of this dive site. There are exciting discoveries to be made

This is the scene at Silver Caves as it used to look when thousands of silversides inhabited the grottos. (Photo: H. Parkey.)

At night, the reef octopus searches for a preferred dish of mollusks on the reef at Silver Caves. (Photo: J. Leek.)

here and photographers can have some interesting challenges. Many of the nocturnal or light-sensitive animals can be found here during the day time. A flashlight will reveal many brittle starfish and sea urchins waiting for sunset in their cave hiding places. It will also turn what normally appears as a black hole into a brilliantly colored grotto. Red and orange encrusting sponges and moss animals carpet the sides and ceilings of the grottos. Some searching among the richly colored surfaces may lead to discovering basket starfish and some rare sponges in shallow water. Basket starfish look very different during the day from how they look at night. With their arms wrapped around their round bodies, they form thin, white disks. Cave ceilings are an especially favorite resting place for these animals.

Few people have seen and recognized sclerosponges. In fact, they were considered extinct and only were rediscovered in the last 20 years when diving made studies of deep reefs possible. These sponges are important reef builders below 150 feet (46 meters) and now are known to also occupy caves in shallow water. Although rare, you can see them at this dive site. Peer into the grottos and look among the red sponges for small mounds of yellow to pale green that have the typical star pattern of the sclerosponges.

Typical depth range:	30 feet (9 meters) to unlimited (wall)
Typical current conditions:	Minimal to strong
Typical visibility:	80 feet (24 meters) or more
Expertise required:	Intermediate or better

Off the northwestern corner of Long Cay, the main reef trend turns abruptly to the east. In doing so, it forms a major point and begins a significant change in reef topography. Well-defined, long coral ridges and sandy canyons run perpendicular to the reef line here and further eastward. These begin shallow and extend seaward to 60 feet (18 meters) or more below the surface. Like Silver Caves, the coral ridges have many holes and grottos that are a haven for all kinds of invertebrate and fish life.

Currents. Moderate to strong currents flow across the reef at this site almost all the time. They are strongest over the reef top and may be entirely absent along the wall itself. Divers who explore the north facing wall of the point may find troublesome currents there, too, and are advised to plan their

A decorator crab wears a garment of yellow sponges that it has carefully snipped from one of many yellow tube sponges at the Aquarium. (Photo: J. Burek.)

Harlequin bass feed on crustaceans that they pluck from the reef. Often, they can be seen hovering near the reef surface in search of prey. (Photo: J. Burek.)

dive accordingly. Currents along the point generally sweep across the reef from the east. To minimize their effect, divers should drop down to the reef as quickly as possible because current strength diminishes near the reef surface. By swimming east at the start, divers will generally enjoy an effortless return trip to the boat.

Marine Life. Named for its varied invertebrate life, the Aquarium is a good place to see the common and unusual. Crinoids or sea feathers are of special interest here during the day. Many of these animals, which normally are hidden deep in the reef elsewhere, are more visible at the Aquarium. A good place to look for them is near the crest of the wall. Their orange or yellow feather-like arms are exposed fully here. Only the small centrally-located body and cirri (attachment appendages) are tucked beneath the coral formations.

Deep-water lace coral and black coral are another common animal along the top 50 feet (15 meters) of the wall. Most extend horizontally away from the wall with their network of branches oriented perpendicular to the slight current that occasionally sweeps the reef.

Fish are varied and colorful at this site too. If you look on top of the reef and in the dividing channels, you can find the usual variety of tropicals. Parrotfish of all shapes, size and variety graze on patches of algae that mantles much of the reef top.

Typical depth range:	40 feet (12 meters) to unlimited (wall)
Typical current conditions:	None to minimal
Typical visibility:	80 feet (24 meters)
Expertise required:	Intermediate or better

East of the Aquarium, on the same reef, lies Nurse Shark Lodge. This wall plunges steeply into deep water all along this section of northern Long Cay. It offers great diving, but this site is singled out repeatedly by dive charters because it consistently features large marine life.

Sharks. The names of dive sites are drawn either from physical characteristics ("Half Moon Wall," for example) or from exciting sightings of animals (Barracuda Point). This site regularly offers sightings of sharks, although I've not seen any during my dives here. The "Lodge" portion of the name refers to shallow caves that riddle the reefs and reportedly are used as sleeping quarters by sharks.

Why sharks persistently visit this location is not known, but elsewhere in the world they are attracted to a particular promontory because of unusually rich feeding conditions that exist there. Whatever the real reason for their presence here, sharks are a thrilling site for any diver who meets them.

Spur and groove formations that dominate here are also excellent for photography of corals, sponges, and a variety of other invertebrates. Reef fish also like the many nooks, crannies, and alleys that make excellent hiding places and predator escape routes. All can be seen here without ever diving the wall.

Reefs all along the north end off Long Cay have rugged relief that shelter shark and a host of reef fish. The dark ridges are living coral spurs that form natural directional guides that lead down to the wall and deep water.

Typical depth range:	35 feet (11 meters) to unlimited (wall)
Typical current conditions:	None to minimal
Typical visibility:	80 feet (24 meters) or more
Expertise required:	Intermediate or better

Opposite a tidal cut through the north end of Long Cay and near Nurse Shark Lodge lies a reef known as Eagle Ray Wall. This area has an excellent shallow reef, ideally suited for snorkelers, and a colorful wall. Here, the shallow reef is an exciting area no more than 35–40 feet (11–12 meters) beneath the surface right up to the wall. A series of long straight coral ridges separated by sand gullies serve as natural navigation aids. Snorkelers following these structures into shallow water are lead straight to the reef crest, whereas divers are directed to the wall going in the opposite direction.

Wall Diving. The wall plunges dramatically into deep water all along this part of the reef trend. At this site the wall is rich with corals and colorful red cup sponges. Here too, many painted tunicates occur clustered on a variety of soft coral branches between 60 and 65 feet (18–19 meters) below the surface. Like the wall at Nurse Shark Lodge, this one is also riddled with many holes and grottos. All are home to a variety of fish and invertebrates.

Eagle Rays. On most dives here, you can see eagle rays in graceful flight just off the wall. Usually, these magnificent creatures are seen about 40 feet or 12 meters below the surface, moving effortlessly through the water with majestic, slow sweeps of their wings. Their regular occurrence here may enable you to plan for some spectacular photographs or video with much depth of field.

Even if rays don't happen by when you dive this site, there are still plenty of good photographic opportunities. Boats anchored here will sometimes swing parallel to the wall making excellent silhouette shots with lots of color in the foreground.

Beyond the wall divers can commonly follow the graceful flight of spotted eagle rays. (Photo: F. Burek.)

Typical depth range:	40 feet (12 meters) to unlimited (wall)
Typical current conditions:	Minimal to strong
Typical visibility:	50 feet (15 meters) or more
Expertise required:	Intermediate or better

Bordered by a wide channel, this site is exposed to a flood of lagoon water and sometimes ocean swells that cross the lagoon from the windward side. Frequent changes in current strength, visibility, and water temperature can be expected during the day, except at those times when the winds are from the north, or northwest. Even when favorable winds exist, water temperatures will change dramatically near the wall where a plume of warm lagoon water escapes in the channel, crosses the reef, and passes over the cool water of the open sea.

The reef at Southwest Cut is peculiar. It is perhaps better suited for a night dive than a day dive. The reef itself has a poor collection of living coral. Instead, much of the reef top is covered with algae, soft coral, and sand. Also unlike other sites along the western limb of Lighthouse atoll, the reef at Southwest Cut is dissected by wide, sand channels that plunge steeply to great depths. It is not uncommon to see the channels narrow progressively but continue until they reach a terrace 130 feet (39 meters) below sea surface. Except for local accumulations of turtle grass mats, the channels are pretty

A steady diet of zoanthid polyps helps keep delicate gills of a nudibranch armed with stinging cells. (Photo: J. Burek.)

Basket starfish climb soft coral near the wall at Southwest Cut and catch tiny animals by spreading their arms into currents flowing seaward from the lagoon. (Photo: J. Burek.)

much barren of marine life. Only the wall with its many grottos and holes appears to teem with life and offers the best opportunity to see shrimp, eels, and various other organisms.

Marine Life. Sometime the variety of life seen at this site can take your breath away during the day time, but the most consistent good diving occurs here at night. Dozens of basket starfish can be seen clinging to soft corals near and on the wall. A varied collection of eels also emerge from their shelters in the reef. Many come to the turtle grass mats in the channel to feed. Others, such as sharptail eels are most frequently spotted in the large coral heads behind the wall. Here and elsewhere on the sand flats or among the scattered coral heads are good places to find scorpion fish, while loads of tarpons can be seen swimming above the reef. This is also one spot where you can find some unusual things, such as the yellow-banded coral shrimp or the sail-finned blenny. You can also get right up to some of the trunkfish and filefish for some excellent photographs. Huge hogfish congregate here, too, and there are always some nudibranchs or Manta rays that spice up the diving at this site.

Typical depth range:	25 feet (8 meters) to unlimited (wall)
Typical current conditions:	Slight to moderate
Typical visibility:	50 feet (15 meters) or more
Expertise required:	Novice with instructor or better

Along the northern limb of Lighthouse, north of the pass to Half Moon Wall, are two infrequently visited dive sites. The southern most one is called West Point I, the northerly one, West Point II. Both have excellent diving, but visibility can drop to 50 feet (15 meters) or less when the winds blow steadily out of the east or northeast. Even during those days, these sites have much to offer because the poor visibility is normally limited to the upper 20 feet (6 meters).

Both reefs have a narrow rim of reef adjacent to a wall that plunges to 125 feet (38 meters). The wall is vertical to slightly overhanging in most places. A variety of sponges and corals decorate the wall with many shapes and colors. Below 125 feet there is a narrow terrace with a gentle slope. Sand and a sparse cover of coral cover the terrace right up to the edge of a second deep wall.

Fish Lovers Delight. If watching or photographing fish is on your list, this is one place you don't want to miss. Schools of smooth trunkfish, all four angelfish (queen, gray, French, and rock beauty) and lots of parrotfish congregate here. Yellowtail snappers are here in great numbers along with queen triggerfish, white spotted filefish, hogfish, barracudas, and tiger groupers. All the butterflyfish feed on the reef here too including the rare longsnout. A variety of creole wrasses, blennies, gobies, and hamlets need to be included on this partial list.

Even if fish are not your main interest, you will find this site a joy to dive. Here, too, the coral is healthy and at least as varied as the fish life. Conch and garden eels are found in the sand slopes behind the reef wall, whereas spotted and green moray eel hide in healthy coral growths that are as varied as the fish life.

Schools of smooth trunkfish scull around the reef at West Point I. (Photo: F. Burek.)

Typical depth range:	30 feet (9 meters) to unlimited (wall)
Typical current conditions:	None to minimal
Typical visibility:	100 feet (30 meters)
Expertise required:	Intermediate or better

Half Moon Wall is an exceptional dive site now included in the newly erected Half Moon Cay National Monument on Lighthouse. Everyone who has the opportunity to dive the offshore atolls should try to dive Half Moon Wall. Here, you can make several different types of dives without moving the boat, and you can take time to picnic or observe the boobie bird colony on Half Moon Cay between dives. It is one of my favorite dives because the reefs are so spectacular and varied. Located on the south side of Half Moon Cay are two striking reef features. First, the coral formations form a narrow rim at the edge of the wall, which in most places is only 100 to 200 feet (30–61 meters) wide. Second, an extensive gently-sloping, seemingly barren sand flat separates the reef rim from shallow reefs along the shore.

As you glide down to the reefs 30 feet (9 meters) below, you will see the reef rim has a spectacular development of spurs and grooves. The living spurs are massive coral accumulations subdivided by seaward sloping grooves up to 30 feet (9 meters) deep at the wall. Many grooves are quite narrow, but easily negotiated by a diver. One of the exciting aspects of this dive is to enter one of the grooves and follow it seaward. A muddy sand floors the grooves. It is easily agitated and can create low-visibility conditions when disturbed. So, lead divers should take special precautions not to stir up the bottom with their fins. Many grooves feature pronounced overhangs that locally coalesce to form tunnels, also known as Grover's Grottos. All tunnels are short and

With their cavernous mouth open, Manta rays frequently make feeding runs for plankton above the shallow turtle grass flats behind the reef rim at Half Moon Cay. (Photo: B. K. Moore.)

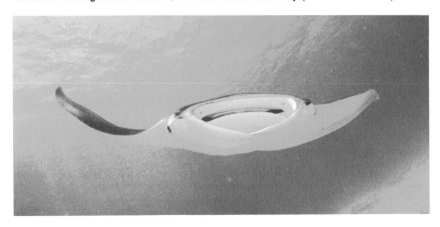

straight so no special dive equipment or experience is needed. As the tunnels near the wall they reach depths of 70 feet (21 meters) or more.

Marine Life. Large and small marine life abounds on Half Moon Wall reefs. It is also extremely varied because of the abrupt and extensive change in bottom types. The sand flats behind the reefs rimming the wall is the place to go if you want to see garden eels, conch, rays, flounders, star-eye hermit crabs, and tilefish. Most of these live on the flats all the time, but manta rays and a variety of reef fish forage in this area regularly.

On the reef, groupers and yellowtail snappers hide out beneath the coral hanging over reef canyons. Razorfish and toadfish are another common site on the reef adjacent to the sloping sand flat. Large pelagics frequent the reef wall. Spotted eagle rays and turtles are most common, but occasionally sharks and large black groupers visit the area. Most of the large marine life is found more frequently along the eastern part of this dive site, as the large pelagics venture in from the open sea to the east.

Garden Eels. One of the spectacular sites all divers should take time to see is the field of garden eels found on the sloping sand flats behind the reefs along the wall. Thousands of eels can be seen from a distance off the western end of Half Moon Cay. Most divers will see their graceful slender bodies protruding from a hole in the sand only from a distance. These animals are extremely shy and getting a close look may take considerable time. As you approach them, you will see successive waves of eels retreat into their protective sand flat shelters.

Rarely seen or photographed up close, the shy garden eel prefers to retreat into protective burrows long before divers can get close. (Photo: J. Burek.)

The beauty of Half Moon Cay reefs is now protected thanks to recent adoption of a natural resources management program. Much support and direction came from CEDAM International and its members who did detailed surveys needed for monitoring diver stress on this popular reef. (Photo: J. Conklin.) ▶

Typical depth range:	5 to 412 feet (2–126 meters)
Typical current conditions:	None
Typical visibility:	100 feet (30 meters)
Expertise required:	Advanced with instructor

Made famous by a 1970 Cousteau expedition, Blue Hole is one of the best known dive sites in Belize. It is a dark blue, circular, deep, depression in the center of more than 75 square miles (195 square kilometers) of shallow, blue-green water. Its diameter at the rim measures 1,045 feet (318 meters), whereas its maximum depth is 412 feet (126 meters). Except for two narrow passages on the eastern and northern rim, Blue Hole is completely rimmed by living coral.

For the advanced diver this site is well worth the trip. You should plan to dive either the north or south side to a depth of 100 to 150 feet (30 to 46 meters), where the shallowest cave features are found. Begin your dive by snorkeling to the coral rim at either one of these two locations. This serves two purposes. First, it conserves air, and second, it provides an opportunity to get everyone making the dive together before you descend. Because your no-decompression bottom time is short at the planned depths, it is best to snorkel toward the center of Blue Hole, just beyond the vertical wall before

Large stalactites hanging from the ceiling of a dimly lit cavern are sculptured by events spanning thousands of years. Divers should know how to read this geologic braille to hear a silent tale of great changes in sea level, fresh water rivers, and island tilting. (Photo: J. Leek.)

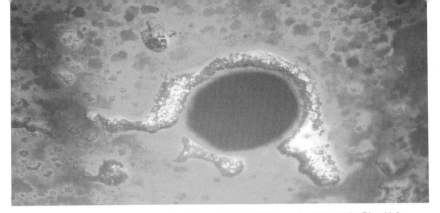

A shallow reef virtually encloses the circular patch of dark blue water that marks Blue Hole.

descending to depth. A good way of maintaining your orientation during decent is to stay reasonably close to the wall. As you descend you will notice the wall crests between 40 and 55 feet (12 and 17 meters) and continues as a vertical cliff to a depth of 90 to 100 feet (28 to 30 meters) before receding at a 55° angle. The resulting overhang forms a cavern ceiling from which hang stalactites more than 3 feet (1 meter) in diameter and up to 20 feet (6 meters) in length. Also found adorning the ceiling are numerous dripstone pillows. More than 50 feet (15 meters) below the crest of the ceiling lies the cave floor with a collection of fallen stalactites, muddy sediment, and an opening to a cave system. Surprisingly, the dimly lit walls of the cavern are covered by a variety of filamentous green algae, boring sponges, and encrusting worms. Little other marine life appears present in the cavern, but the walls above the cavern are covered with cornflake algae and isolated growths of gorgonians. Sharks, turtles, and other marine life may be found here, but their presence in Blue Hole is unpredictable.

Geology. The origin of Blue Hole dates back to an ice age about 15,000 years ago. Enough sea water was frozen in glaciers during this time to have lowered sea level more than 350 feet (107 meters) and exposed the limestones of Lighthouse Reef. Huge subterranean caverns formed when fresh water flowed through the limestone deposits. Since then, the roof of the cavern has collapsed locally to form the sinkhole known as Blue Hole.

Marine Life. Marine life in Blue Hole and on the broad muddy sand slope that surrounds it is rather dismal. Algae and encrusting sponges mantle the walls to depth. Scattered growths of unhealthy stony coral growths rim the wall and occur scattered across the broad, muddy sand slope between the wall and shallow reefs that rim the perimeter. Most corals are heavily encrusted by red algae, hydroids, and gorgonians. The only other conspicuous organisms here are shaving brush and mermaid's fan algae.

The most varied and lush marine life is found on the coral reefs that rim the perimeter of Blue Hole. The reefs occur in only a few feet of water, making them excellent for snorkeling. Stands of elkhorn, club finger, and shallow-water starlet corals, giant green anemones, various urchins, etc. occupy the shallow lagoon habitat.

45

5

Glover Reef

Glover Reef is the most southern of the three offshore reef systems. It has some spectacular dive destinations. All the reefs along the atoll's southeastern limb are great sites with shallow walls, fresh reefs, and abundant pelagics. Middle Cay Reefs, Long Cay Wall, and Emerald Forest are among my favorite places, but getting there requires some effort.

Few live-aboards make Glover a regular stop on their itinerary. Part of the problem is dive sites are not well established. Few divemasters on live-aboards dive here frequently enough to feel comfortable, and besides, there are lots of sites closer than Glover.

So, unless you plan on catching a charter live-aboard to Glover, your best option is to look into one of the two atoll resorts. They are conveniently located, and know the best sites. Perhaps you can dive the Pinnacles, one of the sites that has eluded me on all my trips to Glover.

DIVE SITE RATINGS

Glover Reef

	Novice Diver	Novice Diver and Instructor/Divemaster	Intermediate Diver	Intermediate Diver and Instructor/Divemaster	Advanced Diver	Advanced Diver and Instructor/Divemaster
14. Emerald Forest Reef	X		X	X	X	X
15. Split Reefs			X	X	X	X
16. Baking Swash Reef		X	X	X	X	X
17. Southwest Cay Wall			X	X	X	X
18. Middle Cay Reefs			X	X	X	X
19. Long Cay Wall			X	X	X	X
20. Grouper Flats			X	X	X	X
21. Shark Point			X	X	X	X

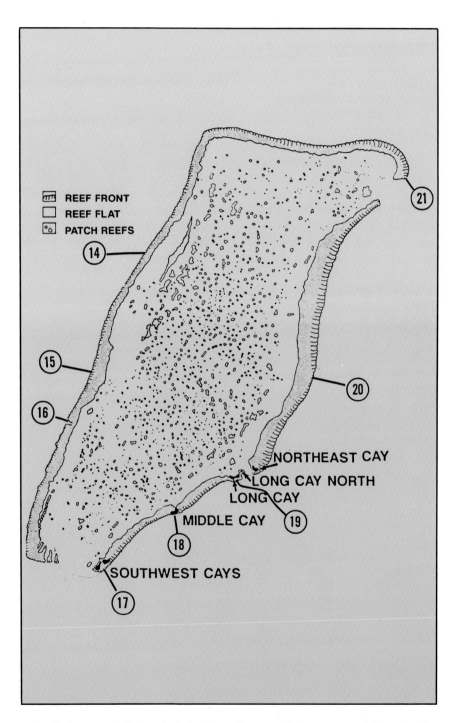

REEF FRONT
REEF FLAT
PATCH REEFS

NORTHEAST CAY
LONG CAY NORTH
LONG CAY
MIDDLE CAY
SOUTHWEST CAYS

Glover Reef has much virgin reef. Most of it is easily accessible from two resorts located on the southeast side of the atoll. (This map is a line trace based on a NASA shuttle photograph.)

Typical depth range: 15 to 70 feet (5–21 meters)
Typical current conditions: None
Typical visibility: 50 feet (15 meters) or more
Expertise required: Novice or better

Emerald Reef is a new dive site along the stretch of virgin reef that forms Glover's western limb. It is located about 7 miles from both the light on Glover's northeast end and from the northern most group of cays on the atoll's east side. Here, the reef slopes uniformly to the west from its crest to a sloping wall. The water is only a foot deep above the reef crest and no more than 50 feet below the surface near the wall. The shallow water, lack of currents, and marvelous fresh reef make this site an excellent place for new divers or those

Magnificent huge elkhorn coral dominate the reef crest of Emerald Forest. (Photo: J. Burek.)

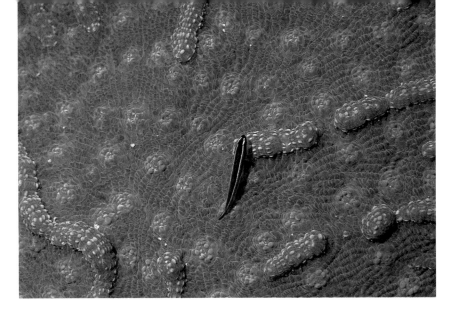

This tiny neon goby has set up a cleaning station on a thin fungus coral. When fish approach, it will ascend to remove bacteria and parasites from its host. (Photo: J. Burek.)

who have been away from diving for some time. Even snorkelers will find this an excellent place because the most luxurious and active reef is no more than 25 feet (8 meters) below the surface. Experienced divers will find Emerald Forest equally rewarding both in the shallows and on the wall.

Marine Life. Emerald Forest is named for its huge elkhorn coral that dominates the reef crest in shallow water. Impressive growths of this coral have trunks more than a foot in diameter and a canopy of branches 10 feet or 3 meters above the reef surface. These stands of huge coral are great places to look for crabs, reef urchins, brittle starfish, and boring sponges when the sea is calm.

Few other corals grow among the elkhorn coral stand, but just a short distance seaward is an absolutely luxurious coral garden every photographer will want to visit. Every variety of stony coral known to live in shallow water can be photographed in this one area. All are healthy and the dense growth of coral life provides ample shelter for many snappers, groupers, trunkfish, and angels. Wrasses and blue chromis are especially abundant.

Divers should also explore the reef along and on the wall itself. The terrain near the wall is a series of weakly developed coral ridges and shallow sandy gullies. On the ridges is a fine collection of club finger, large brain coral, yellow pencil coral, the ever present boulder coral, and lots of forked sea feathers. This growth of animals also houses numerous gobies and shrimp cleaning stations for groupers, bar jacks, and parrotfish.

The wall itself is a good place to look for large lobsters among shingled and platy growths of boulder and sheet coral. There are also large basket, tube, rope, and clusters of sponge encrustations, and a wide variety of small marine life all of which make interesting photo subjects.

Typical depth range:	40 to 100 feet (12–30 meters)
Typical current conditions:	None
Typical visibility:	50 feet (15 meters) or more
Expertise required:	Intermediate or better

Named for its characteristic reef development, this dive site features a profile with two distinct reef zones over a distance of about 800 feet (245 meters). A shallow reef extends from sea level to a depth of 40 feet (12 meters) and a deeper reef begins at 70 feet (21 meters). The deep reef extends to a depth of more than 100 feet at the wall. Between them is a sloping sand flat with a few scattered growths of stony and soft corals.

Shallow Reef. The shallow reef is a photographer's and videographer's delight. A healthy, colorful, and varied growth of corals make this an ideal

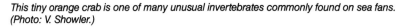

This tiny orange crab is one of many unusual invertebrates commonly found on sea fans. (Photo: V. Showler.)

place for coral close-ups. Magnificent stands of elkhorn, meandrine brain, large cactus, thin fungus and staghorn coral form crowded coral stands. Colorful sea whips, sea rods, corky sea fingers, and Venus sea fans also grace the reef. Movement and additional color are provided by crowds of blue chromis, sergeant majors, and blue-headed wrasse that glide over and through the corals. By looking beneath the coral canopy and into some of the countless nooks that riddle the reef, you can find additional tropicals and abundant brilliantly colored sponges. Because the reef is more than 300 feet (91 meters) wide, a virtually unlimited number of reef organisms can be found. Best of all you can stay here a long time because most of the reef is less than 30 feet (9 meters) deep.

Deep Reef. If you are more impressed by size than variation in marine life, the deep reef is for you. Beginning at depths of 70 feet (21 meters) a mountainous coral mesa towers as much as 50 feet (15 meters) above the sloping sand flats leading to the wall. Much of the deep reef is built by boulder, lettuce, and large-cupped boulder coral and adorned by a variety of deep-water sea whips and rods. An interesting ecologic adaptation to low light you can look for on the deep reef is the development of skirts or platy growths among the boulder corals.

Pillar corals have a soft fuzzy appearance because they are one of the few corals that have their polyps extended. (Photo: J. Burek.)

Typical depth range:	15 to 100 feet (5 to 30 meters)
Typical current conditions:	None
Typical visibility:	70 feet (21 meters) or less
Expertise required:	Intermediate or better

Baking Swash is a narrow cut through the western limb of Glover atoll. Two weathered tree limbs mark the channel on each side. The cut through the reef is wide and deep enough to accommodate only small, manageable boats with a shallow draft. It is lined with coral and no more than 10 feet (3 meters) deep. Although shallow, narrow and remote, the channel itself can be a dangerous place to dive. Wave and tidal currents are not a problem, but small power boats from local resorts use this passage because it is the only cut in the western limb of the atoll. Most power boat captains are very familiar with the cut and speed through it with little expectation of divers exploring the channel. It is really unnecessary to dive in or near the channel because the reefs adjacent and seaward are quite rewarding.

Reef development occurs over a broad, sloping bottom in two zones separated by a sand flat. The shallow reefs grow up to sea level on either side of Baking Swash channel and extend down to 30 feet (9 meters) below the sea surface.

With reef space at a premium 52 feet (16 meters) below the surface, a club finger coral seeks to capture space by overgrowing a shallow water starlet coral.

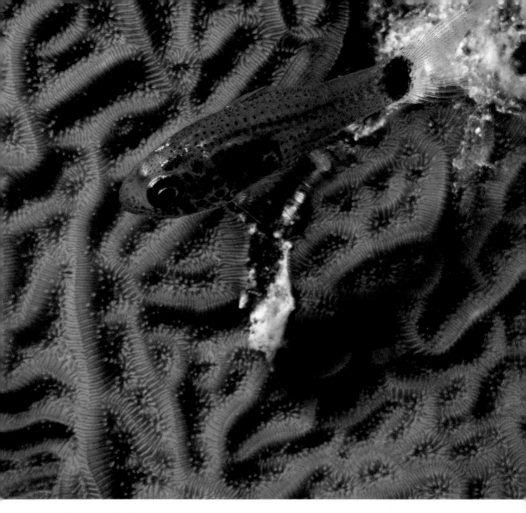

A duskey cardinalfish pauses briefly above a lettuce leaf coral. (Photo: J. Burek.)

The deep reefs are seaward of a wide sand flat that features only a sparse cover of corals. They build up from the sea floor below 70 feet (21 meters) as majestic masses of coral. Huge towers of coral form impressive mounds with up to 50 feet or 15 meters of relief.

Marine Life. Considerable variation exists in the marine life found on the two reef zones. Deep reefs are dominated by huge large-cup boulder coral and elegant growths of deep water lace coral. They are usually not nearly as varied and spectacular as the shallow reefs. So unless you simply want to do a deep dive it is best to stay on the shallow reefs.

The shallow reefs are a photographer's delight. Because visibility is low, macrophotography is probably the best here. Corals are very healthy and varied with most of the Caribbean species of hard and soft corals present.

53

Typical depth range:	50 feet (15 meters) to unlimited
Typical current conditions:	None to minimal
Typical visibility:	90 feet (28 meters) or more
Expertise required:	Novice or better

Squarely off Southwest Cay's east side and only a short distance from the Manta Resort pier are a sloping reef and wall that offer consistently good diving. Both are part of a narrow reef line that forms the southeastern limb of Glover Reef. Depth increases rapidly away from the reef crest before deepening more gradually at a short distance from the wall. Overall the reef

Divers find the luxuriant sponge growth a compelling attraction on the precipitous wall off Southwest Cay. (Photo: J. Burek.)

has little topography. Only near the wall is the reef uneven. Here, wedge-shaped coral ridges are separated by wide, shallow, sand channels. While doing a safety stop at ten feet (3 meters), divers will see all coral wedges border and point away from the wall.

Wall Diving. Like many walls on the windward limbs of the atolls, the Southwest Cay Wall is a dramatic drop-off. From its crest at 50 feet (15 meters) below sea level, this underwater cliff plunges to 130 feet (39 meters). A narrow shelf floored by platy boulder coral, a tangle of wire coral and an abundance of sand occur at this depth. From there, the wall resumes its vertical descent to more than 350 feet (105 meters) below the surface before changing to a steep slope. Submarine dives made here show invertebrate growth is sparse at these depths.

Shallow parts of the wall either have giant overhangs or are deeply furrowed. Graceful gorgonians, wire coral, and some very attractive and photogenic sponges adorn the overhangs, which are ideally suited for pictures with dramatic and colorful compositions. Divers taking pictures beneath an overhang need to remember to plan their pictures in advance so that they can avoid lots of breathing while under the overhangs. Otherwise exhaled bubbles will dislodge enough sediment to make good photography impossible.

Decompression Cautions. Wall diving is an exhilarating experience, but it also means deep diving at Southwest Cay Wall. Unlike some drop-offs elsewhere on these atolls, this one begins at a modest depth and does not allow divers to work their way up to a shallow reef. So divers should check their time and depth frequently and make sure they begin an ascent well before it is suggested by the tables. This way you should have plenty of air left for a slow ascent and a three-minute safety stop at ten feet.

A sea feather makes and ideal night-time hangout for a hungry swimming crinoid. (Photo: H. Parkey.)

Typical depth range:	20 feet (6 meters) to unlimited
Typical current conditions:	Minimal to none
Typical visibility:	100 feet (30 meters)
Expertise required:	Intermediate or better

Located about a third of the way up on the windward southeastern reefs, Middle Cay Reefs are one of the most remote dive sites on Glover Reef. The site derives its name from the small palm and mangrove covered cay developed behind the reef crest.

Most of the dive boats dive this reef, but it is usually a charter rather than a regularly scheduled run. If you want to dive this area, it is best to check with various live-aboards to determine when they intend to go there, or arrange for a trip to Manta Resort, which is a small resort located on Southwest Cays at the extreme southern end of Glover Reef. Even after you manage to arrange a trip there, exceptional conditions are required to actually make the dive. Calm or westerly winds are needed to keep boats from swinging over and crashing into the shallow coral growths of this narrow reef tract. Another problem is large, incoming swells, which are common while storms are blowing in the Gulf and Caribbean. These can make getting back into your dive boat too dangerous for safe diving. But if all the conditions are right, this site is well worth diving.

Middle Cay reef offers some exceptional diving opportunities. A large variety of reef organisms can be found in a limited area because reef zones are condensed on the narrow fore reef. The entire area between the reef crest and wall is only several hundred yards wide. Reef formations are exceptionally lush and healthy in this zone, with few areas overgrown by fleshy algae. The wall, which crests at 40 feet (12 meters) here, is spectacular

Clear water, shallow walls, and a luxuriant growth of coral characterize the reef at Middle Cay. (Photo: V. Showler.)

Juvenile basket starfish stay hidden deep in the reef during the day, but at night they instinctively climb onto sea fans and become voracious carnivores. (Photo: F. Burek.)

and richly adorned with reef organisms. It also differs from wall profiles seen at most other locations because it is terraced at depth. Exceptionally clear water and minimal currents allow you to see at least two terraces without making a dive below 100 feet (30 meters). The first terrace at 150 feet (46 meters) and the second terrace at 210 feet (64 meters) are seaward-sloping surfaces covered by platy deep-water boulder coral. Coral coverage is high and gives these terraces the appearance of a shingled roof.

While crystal clear waters are a delight to dive, they also make it easy to get very deep quickly at this site. Boats generally must anchor so that all or part of the vessel is located over or beyond the wall. Inexperienced divers should monitor their depth gauge closely and begin their dives at the crest of the wall rather than on the wall itself. Plan to enter the water and swim west (toward the island) until you are over the reef near the wall. Descending to the crest of the wall at 40 feet (12 meters), you can begin your exploration of the reef or go over the edge to explore the wall.

Marine Life. Virtually every kind of invertebrate and a wide variety of fish life can be found at Middle Cay. Turtle grass beds with their unique collection of tiny organisms flourish in patches adjacent to the northern and southern shores of the cay. Small foraminifera, encrusting red algae, and hydrozoans cling to the blades of these grasses, whereas several kinds of clams seek shelter among the plant roots. Turban snails abound in the rocky areas bordering the island. Large elkhorn and abundant crenulated and flat-topped fire coral form a dense stand in and seaward of the surf zone. Here also large heads of common smooth star, smooth and depressed brain corals, and yellow porous coral form isolated growths that are surrounded by coral rubble, much of which is coated with red algae. Exceptional growths of tan lettuce-leaf create shallow coral spurs in 10 feet (3 meters) or more

57

Orange crinoids such as this one are abundant all along the crest of the shallow wall at Middle Cay.

of water. Reef urchins, red boring sponges, and many other kinds of organisms hide or live on these large elongated coral growths.

By far the greatest diversity of marine life exists near the drop-off. Luxuriant growths of corals and emergent sponges try to crowd one another. All the common stony and soft corals are found on the reefs here, including some less common stony varieties such as meandrine brain, rare rose, giant brain, large flower, and large cactus corals. Forked sea feathers, knobby candelabra, deadman's fingers and common bushy soft corals sway elegantly on the reef surface. Red finger, lavender tube, giant tube, and variable sponges decorate the reef with their brilliant colors and create homes for thousands of small shrimp, crabs, and fish. The orange sea lily is especially common here. Densities of 25 individuals per square yard (square meter) are not uncommon.

The fish life is varied, but does not occur in great profusion. The usual queen angels, gray angels, sergeant majors, blue chromis, trumpets, and assortment of parrotfish are present. French grunts and blue tangs form small schools of fish, whereas yellowfin groupers, Nassau groupers, and triggerfish prowl about the reef as individuals.

Typical depth range:	30 feet (9 meters) to unlimited
Typical current conditions:	None
Typical visibility:	90 feet (28 meters) or more
Expertise required:	Novice or better

Long Cay Wall offers more than just wall diving. Just off its eastern shore is a shallow reef and snorkelers or divers can enter from the beach. Getting in is a bit rough and a beach entry is not advisable on days with large swells or heavy seas. Fire coral and elkhorn coral grow in great profusion close to shore, but there are some openings in the coral. On good days, divers or snorkelers making a beach entry must look for openings among the dense coral growth before getting in the water. Once past this initial barrier, the snorkel or dive is easy. A large variety of stony and soft coral flourish on this shallow reef. Many of the corals grow in less than 20 feet (6 meters) of water, so snorkelers can see everything.

Further seaward, divers reach a sand and coral rubble zone. The coral rubble is part of a gradual transition from coral reef to a broad sand slope. Between 20 to 30 feet (6–9 meters), this belt is mostly a barren blanket of rippled sand. Its only residents are sand divers and jawfish, which disappear into sand or burrows when approached.

This jawfish posturing near its burrow is one of several attractions found on the sand and eel grass flats behind the coral rim at Long Cay. (Photo: J. Leek.)

Sand ripples die out below 30 feet (9 meters), but the sand belt continues to trail off to 45 feet (12 meters) before ending abruptly at the base of a reef ridge. All the sand is marked with burrows, feeding marks, and a variety of animal trails.

Garden eels are one of several permanent residents. A small group of these shy creatures lives in burrows close to but not in the area of sand waves. Other invertebrates here are alpheid shrimp and various mollusks. All live in the soft sands and are rarely found during the day time except by visiting rays or other fish who actively root for them.

Long Cay Drop-off. Reaching within 35 feet or 11 meters of the surface, the wall is an exciting experience found only 700 feet (210 meters) squarely off long Cay. For seasoned divers soaring over the wall here, there is a vertical drop of hundreds of feet with many overhangs to explore. Everywhere, the wall is mantled with giant plates of sheet and boulder coral below 50 feet. Colorful sponges, wire coral, black coral, and many kinds of hydroids are also most abundant on deep parts of the wall, whereas every kind of soft coral imaginable forms a dense forest on shallow parts of the wall and its crest. Divers who prefer to watch for large animals will not be disappointed here either. Turtles, eagle rays, manta rays, and barracudas are regular visitors all along the wall. No matter what your interest, this drop-off can provide you with many thrilling dives.

Large yellow tube sponges and gorgonians reach out to deep water from the vertical wall off Long Cay to be among the first in line for life-sustaining plankton. (Photo: J. Conklin.)

Typical depth range:	40 to 60 feet (12–18 meters)
Typical current conditions:	None
Typical visibility:	70 feet (21 meters) or more
Expertise required:	Intermediate or better

Another site that stands out along the northeastern reef tract, Grouper Flats consists of lens-shaped reefs similar to those described for Shark Point. It is, not surprisingly, a gently-sloping reef of little relief and home to a large variety of groupers. It consists of two types of reefs, a shallow reef that extends to 30 feet (9 meters) and a very wide, deep reef that begins at 40 feet (12 meters) and extends to 80 feet (24 meters). The shallow reef features mature elkhorn and huge masses of lettuce coral that look like loaves of bread densely covered with a growth of lettuce leaves. These shallow coral formations are replaced by lens-shaped reef masses that are subdivided by winding and coalescing rivers of white sand. Although the reef has little relief, it is riddled with holes and crevices.

Grouper Paradise. Grouper Flats got its name, naturally, from the many groupers that inhabit the gentle topography of the deep reef, and seek shelter within a virtual forest of soft coral and an endless number of crevices in the stony coral growths. They are especially abundant and varied in the shallow part of the deep reef. Nassau, tiger, black, spotted, and marble grouper can be seen lying amid the sea whips and sea feathers.

The colorful tiger grouper is just one of several that can be spotted lurking among the coral canopy at Grouper Flats. (Photo: F. Burek.)

Typical depth range:	50 to 90 feet (15–27 meters)
Typical current conditions:	None to moderate
Typical visibility:	More than 100 feet (30 meters)
Expertise required:	Intermediate or better

Located at the eastern end of the windward northern reefs, Shark Point is one of the more remote dive sites on Glover Reef. Heavy seas generally pound this exposed stretch of reefs making it a difficult site to dive.

Distance and weather play a major roll in determining if you can dive there. The nearest resort equipped with day boats is nearly 9 miles (14.5 kilometers) away from Shark Point. Even if divers are willing to make the hour-long trip to get there, prolonged periods of excessive boat roll are an unsettling experience for most divers. Heavy seas also create extreme boat motion and increase the risk of injury to divers exiting the water on day

Hammerhead sharks have impressively powerful bodies that are accentuated further by a flattened head. These marvelous creatures demand respect and will focus your attention at Shark Point. (Photo: J. Leek.)

Nurse sharks are most commonly found resting beneath coral ledges during the day making it easy to get close to them. (Photo: J. Leek.)

boats or live-aboards. Aside from days with exceptional weather, experienced divers may visit this site by using Zodiacs. Launched from a larger vessel anchored inside the lagoon, these small rubberized crafts could quickly and safely transport divers to and from the reef.

Sharks. When weather and sea conditions allow access to the reef point, the diving is sensational. Sharks, seen almost always on these reefs, are the most exhilarating experience here. Not only may very large sharks be seen, but this point is unique in Belize in its variety and combination of shark life. Nurse, black tip, hammerhead, and tiger sharks may be seen together here on the sloping white sand channels and coral hills. Why they are attracted to this part of the reef is uncertain, but it may be because this exposed point is one of the premier spawning grounds for groupers and other fish.

Reefs. Huge, lens-shaped reefs are sculptured by the constant pounding of heavy seas on the gently-sloping point down to a depth of 90 feet (28 meters). Below 20 feet (6 meters) they are made up of a mixed collection of small living coral colonies and stacks of coral debris. Riddled with holes and spread across a reef more than 1 mile (1.6 kilometers) wide, the coral mounds contain millions of hiding places for a dazzling array of tropicals.

63

6

Turneffe Island

Some spectacular diving awaits those who visit Turneffe. The best part about it is that there are dive destinations suitable for every level of diver. Along the western reef line a few miles north of the Elbow, novice divers can feel comfortable on reefs that are shallow and removed from the steep and deep walls so typical elsewhere. A varied terrain, wrecks, and an abundance of marine life will also capture the attention of advanced divers.

The eastern reefs on Turneffe's southern end are a spectacular place to dive for seasoned divers. Current and walls that crest between 50 and 60 feet (15–18 meters) make the diving here more challenging, but the rewards are great for divers looking to find the large pelagics.

DIVE SITE RATINGS

Turneffe Island

	Novice Diver	Novice Diver and Instructor/Divemaster	Intermediate Diver	Intermediate Diver and Instructor/Divemaster	Advanced Diver	Advanced Diver and Instructor/Divemaster
22. Blue Creek	X	X	X	X	X	X
23. Triple Anchors	X	X	X	X	X	X
24. Hollywood	X	X	X	X	X	X
25. Permit Paradise	X	X	X	X	X	X
26. Wreck of Sayonara	X	X	X	X	X	X
27. Elbow					X	X
28. Myrtle's Turtle			X	X	X	X
29. Black Beauty			X	X	X	X
30. Lefty's Ledge			X	X	X	X
31. Majestic Point			X	X	X	X
32. Front Porch			X	X	X	X
33. Gaile's Point			X	X	X	X
34. Deadman Cay III			X	X	X	X

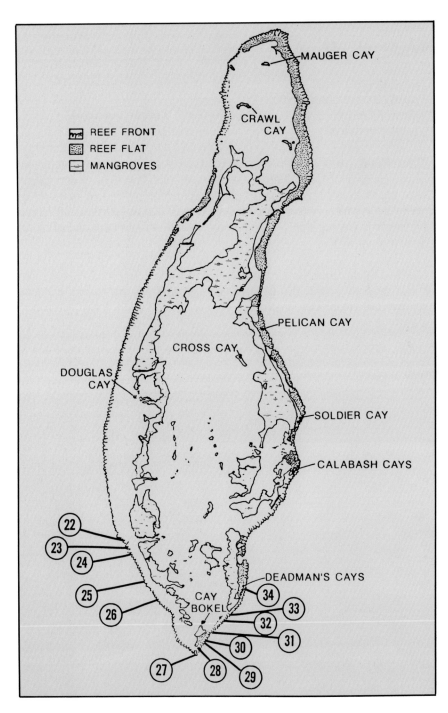

Turneffe Island is the largest of the three atolls and the only one with an extensive cover of mangroves. Most established dive sites are limited to the southern end, but there is enough there for several weeks of diving.

Typical depth range:	20–35 feet (6–10 meters)
Typical current conditions:	None
Typical visibility:	50 feet (15 meters) or more
Expertise required:	Novice or better

Blue Creek reefs are named after the tidal pass that divides a tangle of mangroves at a distance behind the western reef line. The reefs at Blue Creek are shallow, broken, and have an abundant and varied marine life. Snorkelers as well as less experienced divers will find this site very attractive. Live-aboards visiting this site frequently spend the night here and offer this site as a night dive.

Night Diving. Blue Creek has a varied and active marine life, but much of it is seen only on night dives. Crabs and lobsters are among the most exciting and interesting nocturnal creatures. Although these arthropods

Coral stacks surround photographers with a varied collection of subjects. Coral and sponge growths are particularly fresh, but there is also plenty of fish life at Blue Creek. (Photo: J. Burek.)

Spider crabs are among the active invertebrates seen in large numbers during night dives at Blue Creek. (Photo: F. Burek.)

generally forage as individuals, dozens of animals can be found searching for food on the sand flats or coral formations after dark. Most spectacular are giant spider crabs. If divers wish to photograph these invertebrates, they will need a wide angle lens, because their bodies alone are too big for a close-up kit framer.

Decorator crabs aren't as large, but they are plentiful and colorful. These strange-looking crabs attach a variety of sponges to their bodies. None use the same sponges in the same way, so all look different from one another. Like the spider crabs, decorator crabs are active at night. Divers should look for these on sea fans and sea rods, which are among their favorite roosting places.

While looking for crabs, divers may also come across some large Spanish lobsters. These bizarre creatures like to scrounge around for tiny bits of food and are most commonly seen on the floors of sand channels.

Other invertebrates seen here and best photographed at night are brittle starfish and urchins. Ruby, slimy, and Oersted's brittle stars are seen near the entrance of every little hole in the reefs and Suenson's brittle stars draped over sponges are the rule. An abundance of reef and long-spine black urchins complement the brittle starfish. Both shun light and even at night most do not wander far from the shelters they hide in during the day. Although only invertebrates are mentioned here, fish watchers will not find this spot disappointing at night. Blue Creek makes an exciting dive that everyone can enjoy.

Typical depth range:	40–60 feet (12–18 meters)
Typical current conditions:	None to minimal
Typical visibility:	60 feet (18 meters)
Expertise required:	Novice or better

Triple Anchors is just south along the western reef line from Blue Creek. Its bottom topography and coral formations are typical of this side of Turneffe Island, with coral stacks scattered across a broad, gently-sloping reef at a depth of 45–60 feet (14–18 meters).

Anchors. Among the coral are scattered remnants of an early eighteenth century vessel. All that remains are a few artifacts and three anchors, which give the site its name. The three anchors occur along a NW-SE line over a distance of several hundred yards. They consist of two large anchors that are cemented into the reef in an upright position, and one small anchor that lies in the sand among the coral formations. It takes an experienced eye to recognize these relics because they are now heavily encrusted with corals and sponges. One of the two large anchors is easily found because it is only a short distance northwest of the mooring system recently installed at the site. Its flukes are

Queen angelfish are extremely photogenic, but skittish subjects. They prefer to stay away from cameras and divers, so successful photographs of queen angelfish almost always require patience and a dive buddy who will steer them in your direction. (Photo: F. Burek.)

Two yellow mustard hill coral colonies compete for space with an orange sponge(Mycale laevis) *at their base. Even the undersides of corals are valued on reefs where firm ground on which to grow is of limited availability.*

completely buried by coral and sponge growths, but its shaft cannot be mistaken, even with the heavy invertebrate encrustations that cover it.

The other two anchors can be found in opposite directions from the centrally located anchor near the boat mooring. Farther to the NW is the little anchor. The symmetric anchor form is preserved by the coral, but it and the middle large anchor are not the best photographic subjects. Divers wishing to get a good photo of an anchor are advised to find the large anchor SE of the mooring. Its flukes and shaft remain distinctive.

This dive also has plenty of attractions other than the three anchors. Both the fish and invertebrate life are varied and good photographic subjects. Although there are plenty of large sponges and invertebrate groupings, the visibility is better suited for close-up or macrophotography. Queen angelfish are particularly impressive subjects here. Three and four of these colorful tropicals can be seen chasing one another among the coral formations. Most are good size and a few are among the largest I've seen anywhere in the Caribbean, with a length close to 1.5 feet.

Typical depth range:	20–50 feet (6–15 meters)
Typical current conditions:	None
Typical visibility:	50 feet (15 meters) or more
Expertise required:	Novice or better

For less experienced or infrequent divers, Hollywood is a good place to get comfortable diving the offshore atolls. Located on the leeward side of Turneffe Islands, this site is sheltered from swells and large waves. Also, here the reef is wide, slopes gently, and provides ample shallow water diving. Dive boats generally anchor in 30 to 45 feet (9 to 14 meters) of water. It takes a good swim seaward to reach water depths greater than 50 feet (15 meters).

Snorkelers will find they too can enjoy the protected shallows of Hollywood. A swim toward the distant mangroves takes you toward a reef crest that typically has several feet of water over it. Because the reefs are submerged and waves attenuated, this is one of the best places to snorkel the reef crest.

Perhaps the least desirable aspect of this dive site is its low visibility. Although the water is by no means murky, clouds of suspended matter derived from the atoll are typical. Photographers and snorkelers may find this annoying because reefs in 20 to 50 feet (6 to 15 meters) of water are lush and varied.

Marine Life. Bathed in turbid waters, the luxuriance of stony and soft corals is surprisingly good. Here the broken reefs are built primarily by abundant tan lettuce leaf and boulder coral. But flower, giant brain, smooth

Giant agelus sponges form great clusters on coral stacks. Their interiors are a safe haven for crustaceans and small fish from potential predators. (Photo: J. Burek.)

Spiny brittle star and colonial zoanthids on lavender vase sponge are among many colorful subjects that are best photographed at night. (Photo: F. Burek.)

brain, and club finger corals also commonly compete for space among the main reef builders. Less common are grooved fungus, large cactus, rare rose, large cupped boulder, and polygonal corals.

Interspersed among stony corals is an abundance of very large soft corals and sponges. Soft corals such as forked sea feathers, sea feathers, and sea fans form a virtual forest. These corals reach 4–5 feet (1.2–1.5 meters) in height and grow from any spot available both on reef formations and on the sandy floors that lie between the coral build-ups.

Equally impressive is the presence of so many large emergent sponges. Iridescent tube, giant yellow tube, huge vase, and basket sponges are common primarily because their survival during storms is enhanced by reduced water turbulence on these shallow, protected reefs. Emergent sponges are easily broken and destroyed during storms on shallow reef zones, so most sponges living in such environments typically have an encrusting or boring life mode. At Hollywood, these kinds of sponges are also common in nooks and crannies.

A large amount of algae garnishes these reefs and supports a varied marine life. Mermaid's fans grow between coral formations in the sand and are part of the diet of the large gray angelfish. Much coral growth is locally infested with brown and filamentous algae. These algae are important food sources for a variety of herbivorous fish and urchins. You should take time to look for some filamentous green algal lawns because these are fastidiously weeded and aggressively defended by a variety of damselfish. Most common are the threespot and duskey damselfish, which fend off foraging striped parrotfish and divers with aggressive attacks. Many of the more common reef tropicals such as barracudas, trumpet, queen angels, grunts, and snappers are sure to be seen.

Typical depth range:	35–60 feet (11–18 meters)
Typical current conditions:	None to minimal
Typical visibility:	60 feet (18 meters)
Expertise required:	Novice or better

Located along the same reef trend, Permit Paradise reefs are very similar to those found a short distance north at Hollywood. Looking down from the surface after entering the water, you can see abundant clusters of large coral stacks. Most have 10 to 15 feet of relief above the white sandy bottom at a depth of 40 to 60 feet (12–18 meters).

Large, deep-bodied permits are present in mid-water above the reef consistently enough for this site to bear their name. These graceful and fast swimming fish feed in small schools and make a challenging photographic subject.

The coral growth is fresh and varied. Forked sea feathers are especially noticeable because they form a virtual forest of swaying branches. Other soft corals that contribute to the graceful canopy above a garden of stony

Only 4 white antennae give away the presence of a coral shrimp hiding beneath the cover of a fat fungus coral.

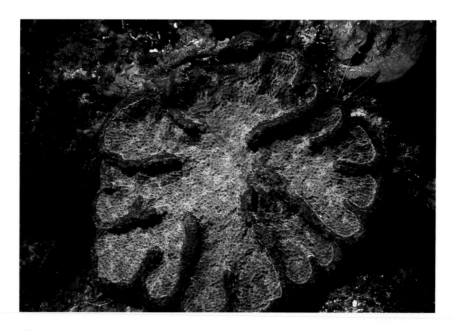

Giant stinking vase sponge are shunned by most marine predators because they are distasteful and smell bad when damaged. (Photo: F. Burek.)

coral include corky sea fingers, deep-water lace coral, candelabra, and scattered growths of black coral.

Boulder and brain coral form the framework of most coral stacks, but large plates of various kinds of fungus coral are common along with flower and finger corals. Together these form a coral framework full of caverns, holes, and overhangs. Invertebrates and fish of all types find these ideal hiding places, so divers can discover dozens of organisms by exploring a single coral stack.

Adding to the spectacle of color and form are a variety of emergent sponges. There are plenty of large basket, yellow tube, rope, iridescent tube, and stinking vase sponges that rise above and compete for living space with the corals. The struggle for space is equally great below where encrusting sponges and moss animals monopolize the undersides of corals and line the walls of caverns and reef overhangs.

Typical depth range:	30–60 feet (9–18 meters)
Typical current conditions:	None
Typical visibility:	50 feet (15 meters) or more
Expertise required:	Novice or better

Sunk by Dave Bennett in 1985, the *Sayonara* is a modern derelict. It is a former passenger/cargo boat and makes an excellent dive for inexperienced wreck divers. The wreck rests on a bed of coral and sand at a depth of 50 feet (15 meters) listing slightly to starboard. It has about 15 feet (4.5 meters) of relief and is intact from fore to aft. Her wooden frame is deteriorating rapidly so entry of the cabin is not advised as the whole structure may break apart. Besides, she was stripped of everything except the shaft and prop prior to sinking. Exterior exploration of the wreck can provide some interesting invertebrate life that is easy to photograph.

Folded back doors and loose metal sheets are a good place to locate a variety of organisms inactive during the day. Basket starfish cling to the roof of these artificial caverns. Typically they appear as pale tan disks because their arms are folded around the central body. Coral shrimp, file clams, and other residents seeking shelter can also be found in these protected alcoves.

Much sediment and rotting wood can be seen while exploring the wreck. Both present potential hazards for the diver. Exploration inside the wreck is not encouraged as bubbles not only reduce visibility by disturbing the accumulated mud but also may cause the superstructure to collapse.

Nassau groupers found near the wreck are quite curious and will allow photographers to get portrait shots without having to feed the fish. (Photo: J. Burek.)

Marine Life. The *Sayonara* rests among some very luxurious coral growth. Away from the wreck, there is plenty of marine life on the reef. Coral growth is typically distributed in discontinuous formations 10 to 20 feet across and about equally high. Sand flats with scattered soft and hard corals and an assortment of algae separate the coral formations.

Most impressive here is the size and variability of emergent sponges. Giant basket and stinking vase sponges dwarf some of the coral formations. Basket sponges 4–5 feet (1.2–1.5 meters) high are common together with yellow tube and bright red finger sponges. Red encrusting sponges are everywhere.

Soft corals also occur in great profusion here creating a virtual forest. Forked sea feathers and common bushy soft coral are frequently seen, along with sea rods and tan bushy soft coral.

Modest fish populations may also be seen. There are always stoplight parrotfish, French, gray, and queen angels. A host of barracudas frequent the area. Small schools of French grunts circulate among the reefs and occasionally peacock flounders rest camouflaged out on the sand flats.

Typical depth range:	60 (18 meters) to unlimited (wall)
Typical current conditions:	Strong (2 knots)
Typical visibility:	100 feet (30 meters)
Expertise required:	Advanced or better

This popular dive site is found at Turneffe's southernmost promontory. Here the reef reverses its direction and is very exposed, deep, and wide. Shallow reefs crest at 80 feet (24 meters) and deepen progressively toward the southern tip of the elbow-shaped promontory. Waters above the reefs typically have excellent visibility, but currents of up to several knots sweep the reefs most of the time. The currents generally flow from the north. However, their direction and strength are inconsistent and should be checked to plan your dive.

Advanced Dive. The elbow is considered an advanced dive because of environmental conditions. Seas are often rough even on calm days because of large ocean swells, making entries and exits more difficult. Once in the water, currents usually sweep divers out toward deep water beyond the reef and 75 % of the dive time must be spent in mid-water because bottom time on the reefs at depth is very limited. Excellent buoyancy control and air consumption simply are a must. Depth, visibility, current, and marine life conditions make this site better as a drift dive and more suited for wide-angle photography.

With their elegant form and graceful flight, spotted eagle rays mesmerize and delight divers of all experiences. Most will cruise in open water just off the crest of the wall. (Photo: J. Leeks.)

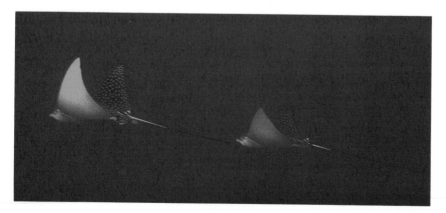

Jacks patrol the water above the reef at the Elbow as they look for opportunities to attack schooling fish, whose attention is briefly interrupted by other predators or even divers. (Photo: F. Burek.)

Large Pelagics. Like similar promontories elsewhere in the world, this site features abundant large pelagics. Large congregations of snappers, horse-eye jacks, and cubera snappers school-feed in mid-water above the reefs. By looking in the canyons, divers can see large groupers lurking beneath a cover of soft corals and rocky coral ledges. Seasonal appearances of shark and kingfish add to the pelagic spectacle. But most spectacular is the majestic flight of eagle rays. Small schools of eagle rays gliding above the reefs are not uncommon and on exceptional days a school of more than 50 brings euphoria to even the most spoiled and experienced diver.

Typical depth range:	60 (18 meters) to unlimited (wall)
Typical current conditions:	None to strong
Typical visibility:	100 feet (30 meters)
Expertise required:	Intermediate or better

Myrtle's Turtle is the first in a series of dive sites on the eastern limb of Turneffe atoll. It is located just a short distance north of the Elbow and directly in line with the old lighthouse platform and two western points of Turneffe. It is among the best dive destinations Belize has to offer. Like the Elbow, Myrtle's Turtle is a deep dive and requires divers to monitor their depth and time carefully. The reef is fronted by a sheer wall that begins at 155 feet (47 meters) and plunges vertically to intersect a slope with a cover of sparse coral plates and sea whips at a depth of about 250 feet (76 meters). Above the wall the reef slopes upward steeply to form the seaward flank of a system of spurs and grooves that crest at a depth of 55 feet (17 meters). Along the wall the living coral formations form huge triangular blocks and an uneven line of ridges separated by narrow cuts up to 35 feet (11 meters) deep. These shelter a fantastic number of different kinds of tropical fish, and invertebrates.

The growth of deep-water lace coral is especially impressive on coral ridges near the wall. Elegant stands of these deep red soft corals can lend both color and form to the foreground of wide angle shots that aim to capture large pelagics. A little seaward and above the reef are schools of fish. Spanish mackerels, horse-eye jacks, cubera snappers, and permits most commonly feed in mid-water, but also present may be small schools of eagle rays, creole mackerels, and tuna. The schools are smaller than at the Elbow, but individual fish are equally as large with some permits in the 35- to 40-pound range.

Deep-water lace corals grow to impressive sizes all along the crests of walls, where they are first in line for plankton swept over the reef by currents. (Photo: J. Burek.)

Turtle. A large green turtle, named Myrtle, has appeared consistently on this part of the reef for the past 9 years. Myrtle is about 5 to 6 feet (1.5–1.8 meters) long and has grown accustomed enough to divers to allow herself to be touched.

Few fish other than the rock beauty and its cousin the angelfish can tolerate sponges as a meal. It takes an insensitive mouth to deal with the glass needles that give rigid support to the sponges. (Photo: J. Burek.)

A coral shrimp tests its surroundings nervously with its antennae as a spotted eel emerges from a hole in the reef where it may have feasted on a sleeping fish. (Photo: J. Leek.)

Typical depth range:	60 feet (18 meters) to unlimited (wall)
Typical current conditions:	None to strong
Typical visibility:	80 feet (24 meters)
Expertise required:	Intermediate or better

Black Beauty is another site along the same eastern drop-off as Myrtles Turtle. Once again, the reef top consists of a series of triangular slivers of living coral and deep sand-floored ravines, which culminate in a straight line near the wall at about 60 feet (18 meters). From there they dip steeply toward the wall and deep water.

The featured attraction at this site was a huge black coral tree found along the drop-off in shallow water. This beauty is now gone. It, like many other large shallow, black coral growths, has succumbed to an unrelenting hunt and demand for black coral jewelry. Rarely are black coral trees now found here above 80 feet (24 meters), and only scattered small trees grow along the steep reef slope above 150 feet (46 meters). Although black coral growths are few, this site still has much to offer. Large pelagics can be encountered all along the wall and more than 40 kinds of other fish can be found among the rugged coral terrain. The ridges consist of beautiful coral growth and have many kinds of other marine life.

Princess parrotfish have beautiful blue markings. They, like all parrotfish, are herbivores who use their strong beaks to help keep the growth of algae from overwhelming reef coral. (Photo: F. Burek.)

An orange sponge provides a soft resting spot for a sleepy graysby at night. (Photo: J. Burek.) ▶

Typical depth range:	50 feet (15 meters) to unlimited (wall)
Typical current conditions:	None to moderate
Typical visibility:	80 feet (24 meters)
Expertise required:	Intermediate or better

The straight eastern reef line south of Black Beauty forms a small scallop at Lefty's Ledge. All along the rim of the scallop are massive coral bastions, and at several locations seaward coral growth creates prominent ledges that jut out above the deep-water drop-off. Behind the arcuate rim, the reef is deeply incised with sandy canyons that slope seaward and spill out over the sloping drop-off at depths of 100 feet or 30 meters. Most sandy strips are relatively narrow features littered with small coral structures, but there is one that looks like a jet runway because of its enormous width and length. This combination of craggy reefs and open sand flats creates a range of environments suitable for many different kinds of marine life.

Marine Life. Pelagics are often attracted to an area because of an abundance of food or suitable shelter. Lefty's Ledge provides both, so pelagics are the main attraction. Perhaps as many as 50 kinds of fish can be seen here on a single dive by exploring the reef and keeping an eye on the

Small schools of midwater fish are common above the reefs at Lefty's Ledge. (Photo: J. Burek.)

Four-eye butterflyfish have a large black spot on each side near the tail. Their tail markings confuse potential predators just enough to allow them a little more time to escape into the protective embrace of the reef. (Photo: J. Burek.)

open sea. All along the sloping drop-off you can encounter schools of horse-eye jacks, bar jacks, Spanish mackerels, creole wrasses, yellowtail snappers, and permits. This is also where eagle rays, ocean triggerfish, and barracudas can be seen along with occasional appearances of hammerhead, black tip, and bull sharks.

Above and on the reef are lots of blue chromis, striped grunts, mutton snappers, black durgons, blue tangs, various damselfish, several kinds of groupers, and the usual abundance of parrotfish. All the butterflyfish are here and a host of blennies, gobies, and wrasses lurk on every coral head. These comprise only a short list of fish found here, but photographers will find it easy to shoot several rolls on these alone and more by focusing on pelagics hidden in reef crevices or foraging on sand flats.

Plenty of other marine life can draw attention from the parade of fish. Near the wall and on the ledges are gorgeous growths of deep-water lace coral and interesting formations of boulder and sheet coral. On all parts of the reef boring, emergent, and encrusting sponges create decorative forms and add rich warm colors to photographs. As you move in and out of coral formations and all across the reef top, you may find large hermit crabs, Peterson shrimp cleaning stations, browsing flamingo tongues, and orange crinoids. Wherever you dive at Lefty's Ledge, your search will always be richly rewarded.

Typical depth range:	50 feet (15 meters) to unlimited (wall)
Typical current conditions:	None to moderate
Typical visibility:	80 feet (24 meters)
Expertise required:	Intermediate or better

Majestic Point is a small promontory formed by a massive coral ridge. Its coral buttresses rise vertically about 55 feet (17 meters) from the steep drop-off found all along the eastern reefs on Turneffe's southern end. On either side of this majestic spur are other well-developed coral ridges separated by sandy crevices. The sand channels generally run perpendicular to the reef line, but some turn and intersect the reef at acute angles near the drop-off.

Like similar areas to the south near Myrtle's Turtle, there are plenty of deep-water lace coral and gaudy sponges on the massive coral ridge. Many lace corals form huge fans more than 6 feet (2 meters) across. These sessile carnivores and filter-feeding basket, giant tube, rope, and other sponges

Divers discover most nocturnal fish and a host of tiny invertebrates by looking into nooks and crannies along the sheer sides of buttresses at Majestic Point. (Photo: J. Conklin.)

A rich growth of coral and sponges make photogenic subjects on the grand buttress at Majestic Point. (Photo: J. Conklin.)

thrive here because they have good exposure to plankton swept along the reef front by currents.

For photographers the promontory is very photogenic and can be the focus of most of your dive. Its decorative cover, divers, or large pelagics are bathed in golden rays by the late morning sun, whereas the point is surrounded by bundles of light when you look upward toward the early afternoon sun. This allows you to capture the effect of sunbeams being filtered by lace coral or dwarf a diver next to the impressive presence of the point.

Typical depth range:	50 feet (15 meters) to unlimited (wall)
Typical current conditions:	None to moderate
Typical visibility:	80 feet (24 meters)
Expertise required:	Intermediate or better

Directly east off the front porch of Turneffe Island Lodge is another site along the same eastern reef line, northward of Majestic Point. Like its neighbor this site has a deep and high relief reef. Its top at 55 feet (17 meters) is about the same depth as Majestic Point, but here there are fewer canyons that extend through the reef all the way to the drop-off and none of the coral

By moving slowly divers can approach an active cleaning station to within several feet. Here a scarlet lady shrimp is seen removing parasites from a spotted graysby. (Photo: T. Starr III.)

A nocturnal predator, the red hind is usually found in the reef during the day. Daytime makes these fish approachable for portrait shots. (Photo: J. Burek.)

ridges is exaggerated in size. Other than this physical difference, little change is apparent in reef development.

Marine Life. Coral growth is vigorous and fresh here. As everywhere else along this part of the reef trend, it forms many protective recesses that shelter a host of large and small creatures. Fish are quite prolific on Front Porch reef and several curious forms may be discovered within the darkened nooks.

One resident found here but not particularly common elsewhere in the Caribbean is a dark blue toadfish. Its body is completely covered with white or light blue spots except around the eyes where a series of short lines highlight the eye with a star pattern. Some divemasters in the area erroneously identify this fish as a stargazer, but its bearded large mouth, body shape, and the sound it makes distinguish it as a species of toadfish. Many divers who have not seen this fish here have heard its distinctive croaking noise, similar to yet different from the grunting noise made by grouper. Although a shy fish, some divemasters have managed to coax it out of its hiding place to give photographers a most rewarding memento of the reef.

Typical depth range:	45 feet (14 meters) to unlimited (wall)
Typical current conditions:	None to moderate
Typical visibility:	80 feet (24 meters)
Expertise required:	Intermediate or better

Gailes Point is one of those dive sites along the eastern reef line that has everything. Here the reef line sweeps inward toward the lagoon and forms a shallow crescent several hundred yards or meters across and perhaps 50 yards (45 meters) deep. On either side of the reentrant is a massive coral ridge that forms a distinctive point. The reef top slopes seaward gently from a depth of 45 feet (14 meters). Its terrain consists of poorly defined spurs and grooves that coalesce and become increasingly more rugged near the drop-off.

A luxurious growth of yellow pencil coral and soft coral characterize the shallow reef. (Photo: J. Burek.)

A scrawled filefish sculls above the reef at night. It is one of many interesting attractions at Gailes Point. (Photo: F. Burek.)

Caverns and Ledges. All along and near the drop-off are many overhangs and caverns. Several good size caverns can be found at a depth of 70 feet (21 meters) on the northern coral ridge, which flanks the recessed reef line. These shelter large groupers and nurse sharks measuring a little more than 6 feet or about 2 meters long. This part of the reef may well be one of the sites where groupers come to mate. Certainly a large number and good size Nassau, black, tiger, and marble groupers can be seen here in early December.

Other Attractions. The broad sand flats behind the reefs along the drop-off may also be a feeding area for spotted eagle rays looking for crustaceans. Small schools of these graceful animals can be encountered sweeping over the reef top toward the sand flats, but more commonly they thrill divers who look for them all along the drop-off in 60 feet (18 meters) of water. The drop-off is a superb place for working with a model to shoot exciting "diver-with-spotted eagle-ray" shots.

Although the presence of large pelagics can be totally consuming during a dive, this site has much more to offer. The stony coral is especially well developed here, and some of the narrow dark crevices are crowded with sponges and soft coral. Clusters of bryozoans, encrusting sponges, and tunicates are other great photo subjects under ledges and on the shadowed walls of crevices. On the reef top, filefish, butterflyfish, and trumpetfish find the abundant reef recesses comforting.

Deep parts of the reef offer still more variety. Thickets of deep-water lace coral, scattered growths of black coral, and scroll coral grace the sloping drop-off below 60 feet (18 meters). The soft coral growths are also a good place to find some unusual photographic subjects, such as deep-water starfish.

From bottom to top, this reef has enough attractions to satisfy even the most discriminating diver. One dive simply is not sufficient to capture all that is here.

Typical depth range:	40–70 feet (12–21 meters)
Typical current conditions:	None to occasionally moderate
Typical visibility:	80 feet (24 meters)
Expertise required:	Intermediate or better

Deadman Cay III lends its name to reefs due east off the northern end of the island. The site is very accessible when the wind is out of the north or west, but photographers will want to dive here when winds are down or blowing gently from directions other than across the mangrove-covered interior of the atoll. Here the reef tract is narrow and close to mangrove swamps, so winds from the west or north commonly drive murky lagoon waters across the reef and cause poor visibility conditions. However, when weather conditions are right Deadman Cay III reefs can be a photographer's delight, because a little bit of everything is found here.

There are shallow reefs at a depth of 35 to 50 feet (11–15 meters), a steep wall, lots of soft and stony coral, and a varied fish population.

Soft corals, though animals, are much like trees on land in that they create lofty perches and homes for many other organisms. Photographers looking for unusual small animals will do well by examining the soft coral cover on all reefs. (Photo: J. Conklin.)

Shrimp come out at night to feed and may be found trying to avoid becoming fish bait by perching on soft corals. (Photo: F. Burek.)

Shallow Reef. The shallow reef has a subdued topography on a gentle slope. It is covered almost completely by coral stacks and a forest of forked sea feathers. Small arches, overhangs and caverns formed by elegant coral growths offer protection to all kinds of animals among the more developed coral structures. Photographers looking beneath and inside shelters will find a variety of brittle starfish, eels, and fish waiting for night time to begin. A flashlight will help bring out their color, but it will also cause most brittle starfish to slither deep inside the reef as they shun light. File clams are another animal spotted in the shadow of crevices. With their deep red mantle and rim of long white tentacles, they are an especially attractive but, unfortunately, also quite shy mollusk that resists all attempts to bring them out of their protective nook.

Photographers will find the soft corals quite a rewarding place to look for small unusual creatures that try to camouflage themselves among the branches. Forked sea feathers and knobby candelabra support a compliment of decorator crabs, sea spiders, and shrimp, whereas deep-water lace coral near the wall makes a favorite hiding place for suckerfish.

Reef Drop-off. All along the wall are lots of deep-water lace, wire, and black coral. There are large plates of sheet coral and impressive basket sponges. This is also one of the first places along the eastern drop-off where you can find yellow tube sponges for which Belize is famous. You may also encounter barracuda, turtles, eagle rays, and some of the other large pelagics seen further to the south.

Appendix A: Dive Operations

This list is included as a service to the reader. The author has made every effort to make this list accurate at the time the book was printed. This list does not constitute an endorsement of these operators and dive shops. If operators/owners wish to be included in future reprints/editions, please contact Pisces Books, P.O. Box 2608, Houston, Texas 77252-2608.

Atoll Dive Operations

Glover Reef Resort
(011) 501 27 7593

Lighthouse Reef Resort
(800) 423 3114

Manta Reef Resort
(800) 342-0053

Rum Point Divers
(800) 747 1381

St George's Lodge
(800) 678 6871

Turneffe Flats
(800) 815 1304

Turneffe Island Lodge
(800) 338 8149

Ambergris Dive Operations

Belize Dive Center
(800) 938 0860

Bottom Time Dive Shop
(011) 501 26 2348

Captain Morgan's Retreat
(800) 447 2931

Coral Beach Hotel and Dive Club
(011) 501 26 2013

Journey's End Caribbean Club
(800) 447 0474

Paradise Hotel
Triton Dive Shop
(011) 501 26 2083

Ramon's Dive Shop
(011) 501 26 2071

The Dive Shop, Ltd.
(011) 501 26 2437

Victoria House Hotel
Dive Shop
(011) 501 26 2067

Dive Boats

Aqua-Venture
(011) 501 27 7593

Belize Aggressor (110 ft)
(800) 348 2628

Houck Fishing Co., Ltd.
(011) 501 24 5332

M/V Hot Dive
(800) 468 3483

M/V Manta IV
(800) 468 0123

Off-Shore Express (52 ft)
(011) 501 26 2013

Out Island Divers
(800) BLUE HOLE

Sunrise Tours and Charters
(011) 501 22 2195

Wave Dancer (120 ft)
(800) 9 DANCER

Ambergris Snorkeling Operations

Arley Martin
(011) 501 26 2051

Heritage Navigation
(011) 501 26 2394

Rubies Hotel
(011) 501 26 2063

Caye Caulker Dive Operations

Belize Diving Services
(011) 501 22 2143

Frenchie's Diving Services
(011) 501 22 2234

South Water Caye
Dive Operations

Blue Marlin Lodge
(800) 798 1558

Camera Service/Rental

Joe Miller Photography
(011) 501 26 2343

Appendix B: Common and Specific Names of Belize Marine Life

Arrow blenny: *Lucayablennius zingaro*
Arrow crab: *Stenorhynchus seticornis*

Banded butterflyfish: *Chaetodon striatus*
Bar jack: *Caranx ruber*
Basketstar: *Astrophyton muricatum*
Basket sponge: *Xestospongia muta*
Blackcap basslet: *Gramma melacra*
Black coral: *Antipathes* sp.
Black durgon: *Melichthys niger*
Black grouper: *Myceroperca bonaci*
Blacktip shark: *Carcharhinus brevipinna*
Blue chromis: *Chromis atripectoralis*
Bluestriped grunt: *Haemulon sciurus*
Blue tang: *Acanthurus coeruleus*
Boulder coral: *Montastrea annularis*

Cactus coral: *Acanthurus coeruleus*
Common brain coral: *Diploria strigosa*
Common sea fan: *Gorgonia ventalina*
Coney: *Epinephelus fulvus*
Copiose cornflake algae: *Halimeda copiosa*
Coral shrimp: *Gorgonia ventalina*
Corky sea fingers: *Briarum abestinum*
Crenulated fire coral: *Millepora alcicornis*
Creole wrasse: *Clepticus parrai*
Cubera snapper: *Lutjanus cyanopterus*

Deep-water sea feather:
 Pseudopterogorgia elizabethae
Deep-water lace coral: *Iciligorgia schrammi*
Depressed brain coral: *Diploria labyrinthiformis*
Dusky damselfish: *Eupomacentrus dorsopunicans*

Elkhorn coral: *Acropora palmata*

Fairy basslet: *Gramma loreto*
Flamingo tongue: *Cyphoma gibbosum*
Flat top fire coral: *Millepora complanata*
Flower coral: *Eusmilia fastigiata*
Forked sea feather: *Pseudopterogorgia bipinata*
Foureye butterflyfish: *Chaetodon capistratus*

French angelfish: *Pomacanthus paru*
French grunt: *Haemulon flavolineatum*

Garden eel: *Nystactichths halis*
Giant brain coral: *Colpophyllis natans*
Giant Caribbean anemone: *Condylactis gigantea*
Giant green anemone: *Anthopleura xanthogrammica*
Giant yellow tube sponge: *Verongia fistularis*
Gray angelfish: *Pomacanthus arcuatus*
Graysby: *Epinephelus cruentatus*
Green moray eel: *Gymnothorax flavimarginatus*
Green turtle: *Chelonia mydas*
Grooved fungus coral: *Mycetophyllia ferox*

Hammerhead shark: *Sphyrna* sp.
Horse-eye jack: *Caranx latus*

Indigo hamlet: *Hypoplectrus indigo*
Iridescent tube sponge: *Spinosella plicifera*

Jackknife fish: *Equetus lanceolatus*

Knobby candelabrum: *Eunicea mammosa*

Lavender vase sponge: *Callyspongia plicifera*

Large cactus coral: *Mycetophyllia lamarckiana*

Large-cupped boulde coral: *Montastrea cavernosa*

Lemmon shark: *Negaprion brevirostris*

Lion's paw sea cucumber: *Holothuria thomasi*

Long-spined sea urchin: *Diadema antillarum*

Manta ray: *Manta hamiltoni*

Marbled grouper: *Dermatolepis inermis*

Meandrine brain coral: *Meandrina meandrites*

Mermaid's fan: *Udotea flabellum*

Mutton snapper: *Lutjanus analius*

Nassau grouper: *Epinephelus striatus*

Neon goby: *Gobiosoma oceanops*

Nurse shark: *Ginglymostoma cirratum*

Ocean triggerfish: *Canthidermis sufflamen*

Oersted's brittle star: *Ophiothrix oestedii*

Orange sea lily: *Nemaster rubiginosa*

Peacock flounder: *Bothus lunatus*

Permit: *Trachinotus falcatus*

Peterson shrimp: *Perichemenes pedersoni*

Pillar coral: *Dendrogyra cylindrus*

Polygonal coral: *Isophyllastrea rigida*

Queen angelfish: *Holacanthus ciliaris*

Queen triggerfish: *Balistes vetula*

Rainbow parrotfish: *Scarus quacamaia*

Red boring sponge: *Cliona delitrix*

Red clingfish: *Arcos rubiginosus*

Red finger sponge: *Haliclona rubens*

Red hind: *Epinephelus guttatus*

Reef urchin: *Echinometra viridis*

Ruby brittle star: *Ophioderma rubicundum*

Ringed anemone: *Bartholomea annulata*

Rock beauty: *Holacanthus tricolor*

Rock hind: *Epinephelus adscensionis*

Rough file clam: *Lima scabra*

Sand diver: *Synodus intermedius*

Scrawled filefish: *Aluterus scriptus*

Scroll coral: *Agaricia undata*

Sergeant major: *Abudefduf saxatilis*

Sharknose goby: *Gobiosoma evelynae*

Sharp-hilled brain coral: *Diploria clivosa*

Sharptail eel: *Myrichthys acuminatus*

Sheet coral: *Agaricia* sp.

Slimy brittle star: *Ophioderma flaccida*

Smooth brain coral: *Diploria strigosa*

Smooth trunkfish: *Lactophyrs triqueter*

Spanish lobster: *Scyllarides aequinoctialis*

Spotted brown shrimp: *Thor ambionensis*

Spotted drum: *Equetus punctatus*

Spotted eagle ray: *Actobatus narinari*

Squirrelfish: *Holocentrus rufus*

Staghorn coral: *Acropora cervicornis*

Star-eyed hermit crab: *Dardanus venosus*

Stinking vase sponge: *Ircina campana*

Stokes starlet coral: *Dichocoenia stokesii*

Stoplight parrotfish: *Sparisoma viride*

Suenson's brittle star: *Ophiothrix suensoni*

Swimming crinoid: *Analcidometra caribbea*

Tan lettuce-leaf coral: *Agaricia agaricites*

Tarpon: *Megalops atlanticus*

Threespot damselfish: *Eupomacentrus planifrons*

Tiger grouper: *Myceroperca tigris*

Tiger shark: *Guleocerdo cuvieri*

Tilefish: *Malacanthus plumieri*

Trumpetfish: *Aulostomus maculatus*

Trunkfish: *Lactophrys trigonus*

Vase sponge: *Dasychalina cyathina*

Whitespotted filefish: *Cantherhines macroceros*

Wire coral: *Stichopathes lutkeni*

Yellow pencil coral: *Madracis mirabilis*

Yellowtail snapper: *Ocyurus chrysurus*

Index